THE HEALING POWER OF STORIES

Also by Daniel Taylor, Ph.D.

Letters to My Children
The Myth of Certainty
The Treasury of Christian Poetry

THE
HEALING POWER
OF STORIES

CREATING YOURSELF
THROUGH THE STORIES
OF YOUR LIFE

Daniel Taylor

DOUBLEDAY

NEW YORK   LONDON   TORONTO   SYDNEY   AUCKLAND

PUBLISHED BY DOUBLEDAY
a division of Bantam Doubleday Dell Publishing Group, Inc.
1540 Broadway, New York, New York 10036

DOUBLEDAY and the portrayal of an anchor with a
dolphin are trademarks of Doubleday, a division of Bantam
Doubleday Dell Publishing Group, Inc.

Book design by Beverley Gallegos

Library of Congress Cataloging-in-Publication Data
Taylor, Daniel, 1948–
The healing power of stories: creating yourself through the stories of your life/
Daniel Taylor. — 1st ed.   p.   cm.
Includes bibliographical references and index.   1. Psychology—Biographical methods.
2. Storytelling—Psychological aspects.   3. Storytelling—Religious aspects.   4. Discourse
analysis, Narrative—Psychological aspects.   5. Self-perception.   I. Title.
BF39.4.T38   1996   95-19871
150'.724—dc20   CIP

ISBN 0-385-48050-4
Copyright © 1996 by Daniel Taylor
All Rights Reserved
Printed in the United States of America
April 1996
1   3   5   7   9   10   8   6   4   2
First Edition

To all those
who cared about me enough
to tell me stories.

Especially to my father,
who told me more than anyone.

Preface

Middle age makes storytellers of us all. The fabled midlife crisis is primarily an act of narrative criticism as we evaluate the plot and direction of our life story, and sometimes find it wanting. The less happy we are with that story, the more likely we are to buy a red sports car or get a face lift—or join a monastery. I have not done any of those things, but I have become preoccupied with the role of stories in our lives.

And I believe that the quality of our stories, individual and collective, has diminished in recent decades. One does not have to be an end-of-the-world doomsayer to feel the confusion in the air. We are not quite sure who we are or why we are here or what we are to do. These questions have traditionally been answered best by stories, and I believe they still are.

I don't like self-help books, but I may have written one. We are altogether too preoccupied with our fleeting mental states. The more we determine directly to make ourselves happy, esteemed, fulfilled, actualized, and the like, the less likely we are to be so. Act the way you should, and those things will take care of themselves. Sounds suspiciously like what our mothers told us, but it's true.

And nothing will help us act confidently and effectively in the world more than the understanding that we are characters in a story that we share with other characters. If this *is* a self-help book, I believe this emphasis is one of the things that distinguishes it from so many others. Realizing our role as characters with meaningful roles takes us out of ourselves and into a community of characters who share interwoven stories.

My own efforts have been greatly helped by those in the various communities of which I am a part. I wish to thank the following colleagues and friends who read parts of the manuscript and generously offered needed criticism: Dan Allender, Robert Brown, Edward Ericson, Barrett Fisher, Tremper Longman III, Arthur Lynip, Gerard Pierre, and Paul Reasoner. In addition, I have been greatly helped by a series of talented teaching assistants: Tim Morgan, Karsten Piper, Don Osborn, and Elisabeth Sinclair. And thanks also to my editor, Mark Fretz, for both his encouragement and his skill. May all these people receive as much help from others as they have given to me.

Our first stories come from our families, and in this I am greatly blessed. I thank my father, Darrell, for being a keeper of stories. His death after I finished this book marks the end of his storytelling but not the end of his story. I am also grateful to my wife, Jayne, for tirelessly telling our children the stories they need to know, and to Matthew, Julie, Nate, and Anne for being such a receptive audience. May their stories be full of meaning, joy, and grace.

Lastly, I would like to give a special thanks to my Ukrainian friends: Lena, Valentina, Igor, Kirill, and Eugene. And to Jumaa in Mombassa. They, more than anyone, know the importance of good stories.

Contents

PREFACE   vii

INTRODUCTION   1

1. The Sound of Story   5

2. What Do You Know
   (When You Know a Story)?   23

3. Characters Shaping Character:
   Beyond Personality   41

4. Finding a Plot in Our Lives:
   The Search for Meaning and a Happy Ending   57

5. Seeing the World Through Stories:
   Stories and the Shaping of a Worldview   79

6. Healing Broken Stories   113

7. All Stories Are Not Created Equal:
   Stories, Relativism, and Responsibility   139

Epilogue   155

APPENDIX: IDENTIFYING YOUR DEFINING STORIES   159

NOTES   167

WORKS CITED   169

INDEX   175

Introduction

Tell me a story.

In this century, and moment, of mania,
Tell me a story.

Make it a story of great distances, and starlight.

The name of the story will be Time,
But you must not pronounce its name.

Tell me a story of deep delight.
—Robert Penn Warren

You *are* your stories. You are the product of all the stories you have heard and lived—and of many that you have never heard. They have shaped how you see yourself, the world, and your place in it. Your first great storytellers were home, school, popular culture, and, perhaps, church. Knowing and embracing healthy stories are crucial to living rightly and well. If your present life story is broken or diseased, it can be made well. Or, if necessary, it can be replaced by a story that has a plot worth living.

Our greatest desire, greater even than the desire for happiness, is that our lives mean something. This desire for meaning is the originating impulse of story. We tell stories because we hope to find or create significant connections between things. Stories link past, present, and future in a way that tells us where we have been (even before we were born), where we are, and where we could be going.

Our stories teach us that there is a place for us, that we fit. They suggest to us that our lives can have a plot. Stories turn mere chronology, one thing after another, into the purposeful action of plot, and thereby into meaning.

If we discern a plot to our lives, we are more likely to take ourselves and our lives seriously. If nothing is connected, then nothing matters. Stories are the single best way humans have for accounting for our experience. They help us see how choices and events are tied together, why things are and how things could be.

Healthy stories challenge us to be active characters, not passive victims or observers. Both the present and the future are determined by choices, and choice is the essence of character. If we see ourselves as active characters in our own stories, we can exercise our human freedom to choose a present and future for ourselves and for those we love that gives life meaning.

Stories teach us that character, in the ethical as well as literary sense, is more important than personality. Because characters must choose (and refusing to choose is itself a choice) they are inherently valuing beings. Every choice implies an underlying value—a *because*, an *ought*. I do this and not that *because* . . . The more conscious we are about our stories, and our roles as characters in them, the more clarity we have about who we are and why we are here and how we should act in the world.

To name and embrace your stories is to accept your God-given freedom. Choosing is often seen as limiting freedom because selecting one course of action eliminates other possibilities. In fact, freedom only has value if used to make choices that make a difference in actual life. Freedom is useless if we don't exercise it as characters making choices.

And the choices we make *are* important. All stories and all choices are not equal. One of the enemies of story and of a healthy society is an uncritical relativism that says that truth and goodness are entirely subjective opinions, that everyone's stories (and values) are radically different and incommensurable, and that affirming some stories and rejecting others is by definition intolerant. Such knee-jerk relativism pervades our society and is the often unacknowledged basis for the fatalistic shrug of passivity, paralysis, and cynicism.

Such an attitude encourages us to be spectators rather than characters. It cuts the link between my story and your story. Story rejects that severance. It recognizes that our stories are interwoven. We cannot live our story alone because we are characters in each other's stories. What you do is part of my story; what I do is part of yours. Such an awareness encourages shared understandings and shared commitments that are central to a meaningful and contented life.

Everyone, without exception, should be allowed to tell his or her story—even God let Adam try to explain. And those stories should be valued. But unless we are prepared to argue that injustice is as desirable as justice, racism and sexism as acceptable as equality, and hatred and greed as honorable as love, then we must insist on the need for wise choices and on the existence of something like truth. Stories give us the confidence to do so.

But stories can be broken. Individuals and whole societies struggle to live by stories that cannot sustain them. Stories that no longer provide the meaning and sense of purpose that life stories must provide are failed stories. If you cannot convincingly articulate a plot for your life, you are living a broken story. If our society as a whole is directionless, it is because we have abandoned many of the defining stories of our past without finding adequate replacements.

Broken stories, however, can be healed. Diseased stories can be replaced by healthy ones. We are free to change the stories by which we live. Because we are genuine characters, and not mere puppets, we can choose our defining stories.

We can do so because we actively participate in the creation of our stories. We are co-authors as well as characters. Few things are as encouraging as the realization that things can be different and that we have a role to play in making them so. This is possible only if we are real characters, not passive victims or observers. Seeing ourselves as active characters in new and healthy stories carries the power to transform lives.

Our stories tell us who we are, why we are here, and what we are to do. They give us our best answers to all of life's big questions, and to most of the small ones as well. Stories engage me as a whole person—intellect, emotion, spirit, and body—and, when healthy, encourage me to be and do everything for which I was designed. Stories also bring you and me together. We not only exchange stories, we are characters in each other's stories, and therefore none of us can live our story alone.

Seeing our lives as stories is more than a powerful metaphor. It is how experience presents itself to us. By better understanding story, and our role as characters, we can live more purposefully the kind of life that will give our own story meaning.

1

The Sound of Story

> . . . the sound of story is the dominant sound of our lives.
>
> Reynolds Price

> To be a person is to have a story to tell.
>
> Isak Dinesen

> Everyone knows what stories are—fortunately; for it is excessively difficult to say just what they are.
>
> Thomas Leitch

"Let me tell you a story . . ."

These words make up the oldest invitation in the human experience. They are an invitation to human relationship and, thereby, to meaning. It is a gesture whose significance has been largely forgotten. If we think about story at all in our time it is as entertainment, as diversion from the real world. I want to suggest instead that within the movement of story and the act of storytelling reside the best answers we have to life's perennial questions: Who am I? Where did I come from? Why am I here? Who are you? What will happen to us when we die?

If this claim sounds excessive it is because story is so omnipresent in our lives that it is often invisible. We live in stories the way fish live in water, breathing them in and out, buoyed up by them,

5

taking from them our sustenance, but rarely conscious of this element in which we exist. We are born into stories; they nurture and guide us through life; they help us know how to die. Stories make it possible for us to be human.

Stories tell me not only who I am but also who you are, and what we are together. In fact, without you and your story I cannot know myself and my story. No one's story exists alone. Each is tangled up in countless others. Pull a thread in my story and feel the tremor half a world and two millennia away.

Stories taught me what it was to be a boy and then a man, what it meant to be an American, how to be a Dodgers fan, where to look for God and what to do when God found me, when to roll cuffs on my blue jeans and when to stop rolling cuffs. Stories also taught that other people are different from me (but not too much), what to say to girls and to bullies, when to laugh and when to mourn, when to speak and when to be silent.

Humans are natural and obsessive storytellers. We constantly invite story exchanges. "How are you doing?" "What's up?" "How was your weekend/operation/meeting?" "How are the kids?" "Did you hear about Annie?" "You aren't going to believe what happened to me!" Each of these and countless more are invitations to storytelling. They are the currency of human interchange, the net we cast to capture fugitive truths and the darting rabbits of emotion.

Why is this so? This entire book can only sketch an answer, but here is a beginning. We tell and listen to stories to reassure ourselves that we are not home alone. Our fear of isolation is instinctive and profound. Every story is evidence that someone else is out there —and wants to talk. If misery loves company, so does happiness— and every other human response to life. We find through stories that others also share our pain, confusion, hopes, jokes, and little victories. Maybe we even feel a bit of relief that some we hear about have it worse than we do, though we don't quite say so.

Exchanging stories stiffens our courage. If hobbits and elves can survive a journey through Mirkwood Forest for a good cause, maybe we will survive that talk we've been afraid of having. It doesn't matter that hobbits aren't real. Their story plays out possibilities for behavior and outcomes that we are free to weigh as possibilities for ourselves. And if it isn't hobbits, then the family story of Grandma's fight to keep the family together during the Depression will do just fine.

There are many other reasons for our storytelling, not least because we simply enjoy it, but the one I wish to explore at length is the role stories play in shaping and giving direction to our lives. This subject has drawn the attention in recent years of, among others, philosophers, ethicists, psychologists, and theologians (all in the storytelling business) as the academic world wakes up to what mothers and medicine men have always known.

Alasdair MacIntyre, for instance, points out the role stories play in teaching us how to live:

> I can only answer the question "What am I to do?" if I can answer the prior question "Of what story or stories do I find myself a part?" We enter human society, that is, with one or more imputed characters—roles into which we have been drafted—and we have to learn what they are in order to be able to understand how others respond to us and how our responses to them are apt to be construed. It is through hearing stories about wicked stepmothers, lost children, good but misguided kings, wolves that suckle twin boys, youngest sons who receive no inheritance but must make their own way in the world and eldest sons who waste their inheritance on riotous living and go into exile to live with the swine, that children learn or mislearn both what a child and what a parent is, what the cast of characters may be in the drama into which they have been born and what the ways of the world are. Deprive children of stories and you leave them unscripted, anxious stutterers in their actions as in their words. Hence there is no way to give us an understanding of any society, including our own, except through the stock of stories which constitute its initial dramatic resources. (216)

The stories to which MacIntyre refers flow out of every nook and cranny of human experience. The child hears them first at home,

7

then in church and at school. They are whispered in the park and shouted from the podium. Stories lurk in the newspaper and magazines, and ride on the wind of music. They flow endlessly from the television set, and at the movies the stories are fifteen feet tall.

We hear our first and most powerfully shaping stories at home. These stories, for better and worse, lay the foundations of our lives. If included in them are the stories of love, of love for us—at the very beginning—then we are armed for life against hostile winds.

A friend of mine whom I value very much once confessed to a group of us that he suffered in his life from what Winston Churchill called the shaggy black dog of depression. Perhaps I should have guessed this, having admired his many drawings and paintings of dead birds in various stages of decay, some draped casually from his bald head in self-portraits. Perhaps I should have seen depression declaring itself in his gently sad eyes or in his slightly too deep sighs. But I didn't.

And then he told us an important reason why he was still alive. He said that a few years back his daughter had moved back home— pregnant, broke, marriage collapsed. It was a dark time for him. Death seemed attractive. Faith and hope seemed far away. Reasons for going on came reluctantly and without conviction.

Then life offered him one more reason—in the form of a grandson. Five minutes after the birth, my friend held him in his hands, whispering, "Grandpa loves Nick. Grandpa loves Nick." He told us this story with his voice cracking, and our own eyes filled with tears. "Nick was sent into the world to keep me alive," he said. "Whenever I felt despair too heavily in the months to come, or thoughts of death filled my mind, I picked up my grandson and whispered over and over, 'Grandpa loves Nick. Grandpa loves Nick. Grandpa loves Nick.'"

You may wonder whether "Grandpa loves Nick" qualifies as a story. I believe it does. These words are the tip of an iceberg, the breaking into breath of years of pain and perseverance. They are a brief irruption into language of a story that had more often been articulated with his artist's hand.

But I will claim more. These three words, "Grandpa loves Nick," are by themselves a story—compressed, unadorned, unelaborated—but a story vibrating with the power of a splitting nucleus. They have everything required—a speaker, a listener, an action, a message, and a heart on fire.

Could Nick have had a better welcome into the world? Do you doubt that this story formed him over the months, and forms him still? Don't you wish such stories for every newborn baby, for every child, for yourself? This story shaped teller and hearer alike, as all our stories do.

But it is only one story, and one that some never hear. While very young and in the home we also begin hearing and inhaling the stories from a world larger than our own: Jack and the Beanstalk, the Three Pigs and the Big Bad Wolf, Cinderella, and Paul Bunyan for some children. These and also the Magic Tignon, the Spider Woman, and the Signifying Monkey for others.

And we know these stories do more than calm little children before bed. We know they are filled with good and evil, trolls and princes, shoulds and shouldn'ts, heroes and traitors, laughter and tears, manliness and womanliness, the divine and the demonic, the wise and the very, very foolish. In hearing them, long before we can read for ourselves, we get early inklings about life's possibilities. We learn that we, like the three pigs, have choices, and that those choices have consequences. We discover that if a bearded little gnome offers a deal that is too good to be true, it probably is. We play with the possibility of our someday being as brave as the boy who plucked the feather from the eagle, or as the girl who threw water on the witch. (If that witch's wickedness can be melted away, might not the evil in our own lives be less potent than it seems?)

And if, by chance, no one tells or reads us these stories, there are always the parallel family stories of princess aunts and troll uncles. Most of my family stories came from my father, a man who perhaps enjoyed telling stories of his youth more than he did living the less exciting one of middle age. One of them was about the first time in his life he thought he might get rich. (It wasn't the last time but it set the pattern.)

About the time Hitler was invading Poland, my father was attending a little church-supported college in small-town Kentucky and contemplating becoming a soap baron. Seems he was returning one Sunday from singing in a gospel quartet in the Appalachians. They stopped to fix a flat tire in front of a small, mountain soap-making factory. (I am not sure if they really had a flat tire or if my imagination just added that, but that's how family stories are.)

Somehow or other they got to talking with the owner of the factory and next thing they knew they were soap salesmen. They loaded up the car with so much soap the back bumper was only inches off the ground, and, hood ornament pointed skyward, they headed up the road.

They found that war-rationing America was eager for soap. They sold all they had around town in just a few days. It was too easy to believe. They started making plans—talking national territories, color-coding maps, projecting, estimating, and extrapolating. They wondered about the need for finishing college. They discussed which of their college mates they would hire and which they wouldn't.

In their determination to do things right, they decided to solicit testimonials. They went back to one of their first customers, the godly wife of the college's most prominent Bible professor. Her recommendation would go a long way with the other women of the town. She greeted them at the door with a smile. "Yes, the soap seems to get things very clean," she said. "But I'm wondering if this is normal." With that she held out her hands, revealing bright red skin that ended at her wrists, as though she were wearing tight, scarlet gloves. My father looked at his friend and knew that owning the rights to California didn't mean as much as it had the day before.

A funny-sad story, but how did it shape me? Perhaps not at all when I first heard it. Perhaps I was mildly bored at first telling, wanting to get on with being a teenager rather than listening to another of my dad's stories. But whatever the _immediate_ impact of this and other stories, I am convinced that stories go somewhere to roost, somewhere deep inside our spirits. They settle there, beyond consciousness, to grow, blend with other stories and experiences, and work their influence from below, subject only to the distant call of memory.

I, the adult rememberer, speculate now that this story told me certain things that were less clear to me before its telling. It presented to me the startling possibility that my father may once have been young, my age even. It suggested he knew something about failure, about receding and atrophied dreams. And the way he told the story—slowly, with gaps between the sentences as he relived it in his mind, and with a concluding weary laugh and shake of the head—implied that the story was not over, that this was only a chapter in a longer, uncompleted story.

In sum, this brief story suggested to me that maybe my father understood more things than I thought at the time—including me. Maybe my own confusion was not unique. Perhaps _my_ story in that uncertain period was a tributary of a larger one.

Am I really ready to argue that I or my life would have been any different if I had never heard about the collapse of the soap empire? No, not for lack of this one story. But remove a second, and a third, and maybe a dozen or two more, and, yes, my life would be different and my resources less. Like the poet Albert Ríos, I am thankful for a "language-rich, story-fat upbringing" (868). Stories, like mother's milk, are filled with the nutrients from which lives grow.

Our families tell us our first stories, but eventually the stories of the family are joined by stories from other tellers. School is another great childhood storyteller. Education exists to transmit the core of the accumulated wisdom and values of the culture. This is an essentially conservative (in the sense of conserving) mission. Not until fairly late in the educational process do we encourage significant questioning of the culture's values, and that questioning is itself part of the tradition.

If cultural conservation is the fundamental mission of education, story is its fundamental medium. Story tangles in its web the particulars of human experience past, offering it to us compellingly in the present, giving us our best hope for surviving into the future. The philosopher William James said the greatest gap that exists in the universe is that between one human mind and another. Flying to other planets is child's play compared to crossing the light-years between the galaxy of your mind and the galaxy of mine. Story can be such a time traveler.

Story is our best hope for flying over the chasms that separate individuals, races, genders, ages (and ages), cultures, classes, and the myriad other differences that render us unique (and potentially lonely). We are told many of these chasm-leaping stories in school. All the academic disciplines, and preeminently the humanities, are in the storytelling business. It is no accident that the first formal mastery we demand of children is reading. There are too many stories to tell aloud. We must equip children with the tools to excavate stories for themselves.

I remember some of the stories of my early education very well. Others have sunk below the surface and thereby become all the more powerful. Dick and Jane taught me how to read. And a lot more. Dick and Jane, and many after them, taught me what Janes should do when they grew up, and what I shouldn't do when I scratched my knee. They taught me what Americans look like, and how they talk. They taught me to obey people who were older and wiser.

And after Dick and Jane taught me to read, other characters taught me a story called American history—about how my country began, and how it was settled, and why that was a good thing, and how I could do my part. They offered me a story called literature and another called art, and two specially coded stories called arithmetic and science. From these many stories I learned about axes and cherry trees, thankful Pilgrims, heroic rides, shots heard round the world, circled wagon trains, inventors of cotton gins, freers of slaves, writers of poems, painters of paintings, wars to defeat tyrants, and something about fulcrums that could move the world.

I am grateful that someone thought enough of me to tell me these stories. If I now know, or think I know, that some of those stories were distortions, or unfair, or covered up evil, that is only because I kept listening, discovering other stories that should have been told me before. The best antidote to incomplete or faulty stories is more stories from different tellers.

After I first began hearing the stories of the family, but before I was taught the stories of school, I was initiated into stories of faith. Fewer people today are brought up in these stories than in the past, but no collection of stories has been as influential in shaping half the world's culture.

God's mark was put on me early and stories were the branding iron. Don't do what God says and you will end up in a whale's belly; stay on his side and waters will part and bread drop out of the sky. Good people get water out of rocks, chariot rides to heaven, angelic release from prison, children raised from the dead, and all their sins forgiven. Bad people get flies, boils, hail, and the death of their firstborn; are swallowed up in cracks in the ground; fall dead while lying to apostles; and, nightmare of nightmares, burn forever in a lake of fire.

If I see these things somewhat differently now, it is not because I reject these stories, but because I read them with different eyes. These stories not only occasionally scared me into being good, they reassured me that someone was in charge of this world; that someone cared about me; that things were going to work out, for me and for the world, in the long run. In short, they whispered to me that I was loved and didn't need to be afraid. That simple message came to me in stories and its effect is beyond calculation.

If many have no place for the stories I heard in church, it is because they have thrown in their lot with different, and no less risky, story lines. Though we are all shaped by stories, we are not all shaped by the same stories. The *relative* homogeneity of the stories of early childhood explodes into the colliding constellations of stories in a public, pluralistic society. Colliding stories suffuse our more intractable public quandaries: liberal versus conservative, pro-choice versus pro-life, environment versus jobs, rights versus responsibilities, watching the big game versus walking together in the park. They often seem intractable because internalized stories are almost indestructible, essentially impervious to abstract reason, threat, evidence, and bribe. Getting me to give up the stories that created me requires a replacement story of overwhelming power.

In a decentered and relativistic society such as ours, we are in danger of losing the social glue of shared stories. This is one of the more important but less remarked-on facts of our national struggle against decline. A social group, of any size, that ceases to share common stories courts disintegration.

We do, of course, have a common storyteller in our midst. Mine was the first generation to grow up listening, and we are different because of it. Television is the only universally shared source of stories left in our society. It spills out hundreds of stories a day, some of which become fleetingly the raw material of our daily discourse together. At its best, such as in the coverage of John Kennedy's funeral, or the first landing on the moon, or the fall of the Berlin Wall, it gathers us together around the communal campfire for an experience together that we cannot have alone. It gives us the powerful, defining experience of a shared story that at least momentarily makes us feel our likeness more keenly than our difference.

At its more common worst, television (and its pop-culture cousins) gives us pseudo-stories—thin, disposable, degrading, mercenary, numbing. Television believes so little in its own stories that it often provides fake, electronic audience responses. The laugh track is television's ultimate show of contempt both for its performers and for its audience, reminiscent of Mark Twain's description of the incompetent teller of a comic story: "And sometimes, if he has had good success, he is so glad and happy that he will repeat the 'nub' of it and glance around from face to face, collecting applause, and then repeat it again. It is a pathetic thing to see" (1359).

It may well be an important sign of our deterioration as a society that most of our shared stories come from television, but there is no denying its centrality. One young man I know grew up in a home in which television was sternly forbidden on religious grounds. So alienated did he feel by being unable to speak the language of current television shows that he made it a point to listen closely to playground conversation about the latest television story lines in the morning, so that in the afternoon he could pretend to have seen the shows when talking with friends. Not knowing the shared stories literally leaves one mute, unable to join the human conversation.

These are perhaps our most important sources of stories—family, education, religion, and popular media. MacIntyre says, "Deprive children of stories and you leave them unscripted, anxious stutterers in their actions as in their words." If young people seem directionless and bored today, and we with them, it may reflect a decline in the quality of our common stories. We are less certain stories have meaningful endings, much less happy ones. We therefore are more inclined to think happiness and significance can be bought when in fact they can only be discovered, and, in a limited way, created.

But what, after all these claims, is a story, anyway? Let me hazard a tentative definition, recognizing that most definitions leak. _A story is the telling of the significant actions of characters over time._ Let us look briefly at each element of this definition, saving fuller discussion for later.

There is no story until there is a telling. Although I myself often refer to the pain of people whose stories are never told—individuals and entire groups—I wonder if the phrase "untold stories" is not a contradiction in terms. They are, I think, only events, experiences, disconnected accidents of circumstance, until a teller gives them shape, connects the dots, weaves the random threads of experience into the discernible pattern of story. (I would insist, of course, that people can be their own storytellers, not requiring others to articulate or validate their stories.)

It is the _telling_ aspect of story that first marks its humanity. A teller implies someone with something to say who believes that someone else, somewhere, wants to hear it. Many a story is sent out into the world as an act of faith. "Here is what has happened to me or to those I love. Here is what I think, what I feel, what I imagine. Does anyone care? Is anyone listening?"

Stories need only a teller to exist, but every storyteller hopes for a listener. (The teller can also serve as an audience of one, but that takes away much of the significance and almost all the fun.) I think Robert Frost had something like this in mind in his poem "The Pasture" (the poem he chose to be first in his collected poems):

> *I'm going out to clean the pasture spring;*
> *I'll only stop to rake the leaves away*
> *(And wait to watch the water clear, I may)*
> *I sha'nt be gone long.—You come too.*
>
> *I'm going out to fetch the little calf*
> *That's standing by the mother. It's so young*
> *It totters when she licks it with her tongue.*
> *I sha'nt be gone long.—You come too.*

This is the essential invitation of story: "You come too." In this invitation resides its formative and healing powers: "Join me in my experience. Let's go through this together. What has been true (or painful, or beautiful, or good, or puzzling) for me might be so for you." It is a seductive invitation. We are flattered, even if only unconsciously, to be included in such a dialogue, and it doesn't matter whether the teller knows we exist.

Stories encourage in the listener an attitude of belief. We are perfectly happy for an ox to be blue, for straw to be spun into gold, for one warrior to defeat a dozen (smiling to boot), for the sun to stop or turn to blood, for wise gnomes in other galaxies to have Einstein's eyes and great wisdom.

But these are mere details of plot. More importantly, we are, when under the spell of some stories, willing to believe that good is more powerful than evil, that death is preferable to dishonor, that perseverance pays, that truth is more than a word and justice more than a definition of the powerful, that love exists—if only in the cracks. And if we believe all this, and much more, while the story is being told, we do not abandon that belief entirely when we return to our own personal stories.

If stories require telling, they also require something to tell. And not just any something, but something that is worth the telling. Even skillful and detailed descriptions of objects, people, and actions do not necessarily make a story, any more than a security camera in a bank lobby necessarily creates a film. What is required are circumstances or events that matter.

What, then, matters? A brief answer is anything that reveals or explores our humanity. What matters, among other things, is a human encounter with and response to pain, happiness, evil, boredom, love, hate, grace, violence, goodness, greed, God, laughter, spite, and on and on.

A sequence of events does not itself make a story. The novelist E. M. Forster made a famous observation about plot. "The king died and then the queen died" (86) is, Forster says, merely a temporal sequence of events: "the chopped-off length of the tapeworm of time" (85). "The king died, and then the queen died of grief" is a plot, what we are calling a story. All our interest in stories resides in "of grief." There lies human motivation, character, psychology, values, aspirations, and the like. In my father's story of the failed soap empire, what is interesting is not that the soap turned out to be worthless, but that they didn't see it coming. In a thoroughly human way, they built dream castles without earthly foundations.

One criterion by which we judge the significance of actions, in a story or in our lives, is whether or not they change us. A genuine story will not leave us alone. It insists, sometimes in the most impolite terms, on changing us. Not necessarily cataclysmic, life-redirecting change, but change nonetheless.

I believe, for instance, that my life took a slight but perceptible change in direction in my late teens from reading J. R. R. Tolkien's

The Lord of the Rings. Trolls, elves, hobbits, wizards, dark woods, forest havens, caves, mountain strongholds, treachery, cowardice, courage, perseverance—what have these to do with being a teenager in California during the Vietnam War?

Nothing and everything. I found embodied in that fantasy what every teenager needs to find—especially one coming of age in the moral ambiguity of the late 1960s: that there is a difference between good and evil, that the distinction is usually clear enough to act on, that fighting for good is worthwhile even if one loses, that average, even unimpressive, people can do so, and, farfetched as it may seem, that good eventually wins out in the end—though not without lingering wounds.

I purposed quite consciously to try to be on the side of good in life, to the extent that I could discern it, and to take chances to see that it prevailed. If I was too embarrassed by that kind of idealism to say so then, and if that seems to me an even greater leap of faith now, I still do not think such a conviction, rising from an encounter with such a story, has been without consequences. If the change in direction was small at the time, it may have been one that, like a small, early course correction in a planetary probe, has made a larger difference in where I am many years later.

The impact of stories on who we are leads us to the third element of my definition of story—character. Significant action in stories flows through characters. And characters, no matter how furry or many-legged or leafy or otherworldly, are in the final analysis human. In our creaturely egoism, we delight in stories about ourselves —and every story is.

What is a character? A character is a bundle of values in action. It is Macbeth with a knife in his hand agonizing between loyalty to the crown and the palpable desire to wear it. It is Anna Karenina choosing between a lover and a son. Character is Tommy Wilhelm finding that steam baths will not cure what ails him, an Auschwitz prisoner fasting on Yom Kippur to embarrass God, Murphy taking none of Mr. Endon's chess pieces so as to preserve Endon's patterns, and Edna walking into the waves with no intention of coming out again. (You may not recognize some of these, but I would guess that even these slivers from stories have prodded your curiosity.)

Characters interest us because of their choices—the ones they make and the ones they don't. The suspense we feel in stories derives more from this element of choice than from twists and turns of external events. And in the best stories this suspense exists even when we already know what all the choices will be. (Every time I reread *Billy Budd,* I find myself hoping that Billy won't hit Claggart this time and that maybe everything will be okay.)

Because characters have choices, stories are inherently concerned with right and wrong—with morality. For all the reflexive relativism in our culture, we still believe in good and evil in our bones and are drawn to microdramas of "ought" and "should." Like jurors, we listen to the evidence, weigh the motivations, put ourselves in the defendant's shoes, and render our verdicts.

In making their choices, characters reveal who they are. They define themselves by the values they live, often unconsciously. A three-thousand-year-old biblical proverb highlights this truth: "Even children make themselves known by their acts, by whether what they do is pure and right" (Proverbs 20:11). Characters in stories also "make themselves known" by their acts, especially those actions that take place between the ears.

That we get caught up in the lives of characters points to the last aspect in our definition of story as the telling of significant actions of characters *over time.* Over time can refer to both the duration of the action *in* the story and the time it takes us to be *told* the story. Each is a necessary part of the definition of story and our attraction to it. Because stories take time to run their course, we can live with them for a while, and they with us. We can adapt to their rhythm, entertaining the possibilities they embody.

Because stories unfold over time they contain the possibility for change mentioned earlier, change within the lives of the characters and change within the lives of the listeners. Without that possibility, stories lose their interest and their power. If the ugly duckling could never become a swan, or Beowulf die, or Faustus regret the selling of his soul, or Celie learn to make pants and accept herself, then stories would bore us. Stories do not require happy endings, but they must hold out the possibility for things being different than they are. (Even the few stories, like *The Sun Also Rises,* that seem to end exactly where they started, leave readers in a different place from where they started.)

In defining stories I have drawn my examples primarily from that special class of stories we call literature. But there is no essential difference between these stories and our stories. The qualities of fictional stories are the defining qualities of our own lives. We too are characters engaged in significant action over time.

Some declare, in fact, that we are drawn to narratives because we experience our own lives as a narrative, as story. Stephen Crites claims that "stories give qualitative substance to the form of experience because [experience] is itself an incipient story" (297). Crites and others argue that the human brain is so constructed that it actually processes experience in narrative form. It seeks to integrate separate actions, actors (characters), sequence, cause and effect (the primary link between actors and actions) into a meaningful whole. Gestalt psychology points out the human passion for order that insists on drawing lines between the stars to form constellations (and creating stories to explain why they are there), and on finding a significant plot in our own lives.

We hunger for stories of all kinds, then, because we are busy trying to figure out the plot and theme of our own story and are eager for hints. Ivan Karamazov helps me understand the part of me that finds it impossible to believe a good God made this suffering world, his brother Alyosha appeals to the part that finds it impossible not to believe. Any absolute distinction between *fiction* and *real* ignores the overlap and correspondences between narratives of any kind—created or lived.

We both perceive and create reality. There is a real world outside of ourselves, but there is also a self-made or crafted aspect to all our perceptions and beliefs. The stories of literature are more consciously crafted than other stories, but they are not different in kind or in their ability to influence us.

The story quality of our own lives is apparent in many common features of everyday life: our love of gossip, nostalgia, and reminiscence; our desire to explain ourselves and our actions—to be understood; our near-obsession with the self, self-actualization, self-improvement; our penchant for analyzing in exhausting detail our relationships with others; our habit of dreaming and daydreaming; the desire to do things that are exciting, interesting, unusual; our limited but genuine love of surprise and the unexpected; our fundamental desire to feel that we are moral; our agonizing over choices; our concern for what will happen next, and for the future and how things will "turn out"; and, perhaps most powerful of all, our fundamental desire that our lives mean something.

Seeing our lives as stories, rather than as an unrelated series of random events, increases the possibility for having in our lives what we find in the best stories: significant, purposeful action. We all want very much for it to have mattered that we were here. If nothing in the universe is different, even better, because I exist, then I am hard pressed to justify my next breath. It is difficult for me to see why anything I am or do is meaningful unless I begin to understand my connectedness to others, to the past, and to the future. That connectedness is primarily the connectedness of story—of lives interwoven over time in a purposeful plot. Understanding my life in this way gives me better reasons than I otherwise have to live life with optimism and courage.

Living our lives is like being in the middle of reading or listening to a story; we do not yet know how it is going to turn out, or perhaps even what the ultimate "point" is. MacIntyre says that our lives are like quest narratives—stories in which characters must overcome great obstacles to find something of great value (219). It would seem one cannot have a quest without knowing what one is looking for. Yet often the quester is confused or mistaken about the true goal of the quest until near the end. The *process* of questing—taking purposeful action—is a necessary part of discovering what the character is questing for. So it is with us. Seeing our lives as stories does not guarantee total clarity as to what our story will ultimately mean. I can only discover or create that meaning in the living of my story. That it does and will have meaning is an act of faith, much as it is an act of faith to listen patiently to someone else's story with the assumption that you are not wasting your time. But though I do not necessarily know the full meaning of my life, seeing it as a story interrelated with many other stories greatly increases the likelihood that it will in fact have a meaning.

2

What Do You Know (When You Know a Story)?

> But in order to make you understand, to give you my life, I must tell you a story—and there are so many, and so many—stories of childhood, stories of school, love, marriage, and death, and so on.
>
> *Virginia Woolf*

"What do you know?" So runs one of the stock questions by which we elicit stories from each other. It is a very good question. What *do* we know when we *know* a story? Do we, in fact, actually know anything? If we do, how does it compare to what we know, or think we know, through reason or other ways of knowing? Are we perhaps claiming too much to say that stories genuinely help us to know how to live, especially if we cannot say exactly what it is we know?

Allow me to begin an answer to these questions with a story I heard told by the Native American writer Scott Momaday. He says that Scott Momaday is only one of his names. Another is Tsoai-talee, Rock-Tree Boy, his Kiowa name. As with all names in his culture, how he got that name is very important.

When he was very small his family traveled from their home in Oklahoma to Devils Tower in Wyoming. This great stone monolith, called Tsoai (Rock Tree) in Kiowa, rises more than a thousand feet in the air above a flat plain. In his novel *House Made of Dawn*, Momaday says the tower was something that the Kiowa knew had to be accounted for before more mundane matters could be attended to:[1] "There are things in nature which engender an awful quiet in the heart of man. . . . He must never fail to explain such a thing to himself, or else he is estranged forever from the universe" (120).

The Kiowas explained it by telling a story, the single best way human beings have for accounting for their experience. A Kiowa boy and his seven sisters were playing. As sometimes happens, the boy turned into a bear and began to chase his sisters. Terrified, they ran to the stump of a great tree which told them to climb up on it. As their bear brother reached for them the stump stretched up into the sky. The bear's sharp claws scored its sides, creating the amazing vertical lines we see in the stone today. To save the girls from their brother, they were changed into stars and placed in the sky, forming what most of us call the Big Dipper.

When Momaday's family returned to Oklahoma from Devils Tower, they gathered with friends and other family to tell of their journey. An old man listened to the story of their travels and decided that little Scott Momaday would be named Tsoai-talee— Rock-Tree Boy—to commemorate the experience:

> In the arbor Pohd-lohk entered among the members of his dead stepson's family and was full of good humor and at ease. He took up the child in his hands and held it high, and he cradled it in his arms, singing to it and rocking it to and fro. . . . And after a time all the other voices fell away, and his own grew up in their wake. It became monotonous and incessant, like a long running of the wind. . . . Pohd-lohk spoke, as if telling a story, of the coming-out people, of their long journey. He spoke of how it was that everything began, of Tsoai, and of the stars falling or holding fast in strange patterns on the sky. And in this, at last, Pohd-lohk affirmed the whole life of the child in a name, saying: Now you are, Tsoai-talee. (*Names* 56–57)

Momaday claims this family and tribal story helped shape his understanding of himself and his place in the world. It tells him who he is. "My name is Tsoai-talee. I am, therefore, Tsoai-talee; therefore I am." The echo of Descartes's famous "I think, therefore I am" is undoubtedly intentional. Descartes said his awareness of himself thinking proved he existed; Momaday knows he exists because he is part of a story that has given him a name. He *is* the boy in the story—they share the same name—and therefore the stars of the constellation are his sisters. He is connected to the universe. No matter where he is, he can look into the sky and feel at home.

Here is one answer to the question of what we can know when we know a story. We can know we fit.

Momaday's Kiowa name, and the story that lies behind it, tells him there is a place for him in the universe, that neither he nor it is alien. He is accounted for, he has a role to play, he is known and can know.

"But wait," the skeptic says. "That constellation is composed of seven balls of burning gas many light-years removed from each other which have no significant relationship at all except one that we make up in order to fool ourselves into thinking the universe is somehow friendly to us. Momaday doesn't necessarily *know* that he *fits,* as you so sentimentally put it; he only *thinks* he does."

He only thinks he does? If you think you fit, then you fit. There are some kinds of knowledge that need no external verification. If I think I am in love, I am in love. If I think blue a beautiful color, it is a beautiful color. If I think life is exciting and worth living, then it is. And do not say this is merely personal opinion, not knowledge, because *all* knowledge is personal—even if some kinds of knowledge are more verifiable than others.

Have you ever driven through what seemed to you like godforsaken parts of the country, passed by little homesteads or little towns, and wondered, "Why would anyone want to live in a place like this?" The novelist Larry Woiwode suggests that story has something to do with it:

> Why is it that mature people who have traveled through nearly every state of the union, and even Europe, choose to live in

North Dakota, and say that it's so unique there are few places like it in the world? You won't know the answer unless you establish the particularity of the place, and the people who lived here in the past, by talking to your parents, who talked to their parents, you can be sure, who even more surely talked with and were taught by theirs, until the generational lines come to press across your forehead, in covenant, like a baptismal seal. (7)

The stories of place passed down from generation to generation render that place unique, weight it with the freight of human experience, and make it companionable.

My father was, off and on, a preacher. We hopped around from place to place and church to church, often staying no more than a year or two. This gave him the opportunity to recycle a fair number of his favorite sermons, and me the opportunity to become quite familiar with them.

One of those sermons had an illustrative story in it that my father told with great flair. It seems this boy had a pot of honey. He was walking down the road and eating the honey by the fingerful. A smaller boy was tagging along, making a pest of himself.

"That sure does look good. What's it like?"

"Well, it's sticky."

"I can see that. I wonder what it tastes like."

"It tastes kind of sweet and smooth."

"Sweet like sugarcane or sweet like an apple?"

"More like sugarcane, only different."

"Smooth like butter, or smooth like milk?"

Irritated, the boy with the pot took a big fingerful and rammed it into the little kid's mouth. "Listen, just shut up and try some yourself!"

My father used the story for spiritual purposes, trying to illustrate something about faith in God. I want to apply it to the question of what we know when we know our place in a story. That knowledge is the knowledge of something *experienced,* something lived out in time and space, whether externally or internally. What do you *know* about the taste of honey after you have tasted it? You do not have scientific knowledge of the chemical makeup of honey, or of the physical process of tasting. You may or may not be able to explain the taste to someone else. But you know honey in a way that no one who hasn't tasted honey can ever know it.

The same is true regarding the stories of which you are a part. Stephen Crites claims:

> The stories people hear and tell, the dramas they see performed, not to speak of the sacred stories that are absorbed without being directly heard or seen, shape in the most profound way the *inner* story of experience. We imbibe a sense of the meaning of our own baffling dramas from these stories, and this sense of its meaning in turn affects the form of a man's experience and the style of his action. (304; emphasis added)

To use the example of Momaday again, he knows he fits because he has experienced the feeling of fitting. Not *merely* feeling, as the skeptic would say, because in the case of being at home in the universe, feeling is everything. If you do not *feel* at home, it does not matter what you think about it abstractly.

Further, as Crites suggests, not only do we experience stories but those stories then help determine our *subsequent* experience. That is, we feel and interpret the raw data of our lives differently because of our previous experience with our particular set of stories. Because I grew up identifying with the stories of the Bible, for instance, where there is ready commerce between this world and a transcendent one, I am more likely to sense (intuitively, rationally, and emotionally) a spiritual reality behind the material one than if I had been raised in the stories of agnosticism or materialism. Stories not only give us ways of understanding reality, they help determine what we are likely to perceive or be blind to—to recognize as *real*—in the endless stream of data flowing around us that we call experience.

Stories, then, not only help us make sense of our present and past experience, they also allow us to imagine possibilities for ourselves in the future. When my children were small, their favorite stories were the ones in which *they* were the primary characters. They insisted on stories in which they were heroic, courageous, strong, and resourceful. They cheered themselves as I described them defeating alien monsters, performing amazing feats of valor and cunning. That they were tiny, in footed pajamas, and snuggling under a blanket at the time of the telling was irrelevant. They could *see* themselves being in the future something other than they were presently.

This ability to see ourselves as something more and better than we presently are is dependent on our story-making abilities, and is a form of knowledge. It derives from the power and centrality of the imagination—the ability to see and believe in that which does not presently exist or is not detectable by the senses. The inability to imagine a variety of future stories for ourselves in which our lives are rich and meaningful diminishes on the everyday level the actual possibilities for our lives.

It is crucial, therefore, that we surround children, and ourselves, with healthy stories. These stories should be filled with mentors, models, and heroes who do the kinds of things, physically and spiritually, that we ourselves wish to do. If I cannot imagine myself doing something, I am unlikely even to attempt it. Stories multiply our possibilities.

I had a mentor in college who encouraged me to imagine a story for myself which included graduate school and teaching literature. It is not a story that had occurred to me before, and yet, because I embraced it, it became possible and then true. This power of the imagination links the past and present to the future, and gives us the possibility not only to *know* things, but to *create* whole new realities.

The great competitor with story as a way of knowing is reason, especially scientific reasoning. For the last three hundred years in the West, science has been the standard against which all other forms of knowledge have been measured—and usually found wanting. Many feel we do not *really* know something until it has been blessed by the scientific method and the kind of reasoning associated with it.

I am not at all interested in denying the power of analytic reason. Nor am I interested in seeing it _replaced_ by narrative or anything else. Life is murky enough so that we need to be open to many different ways of learning things. Those who champion reason, however, are sometimes not so charitable. They imply that their views and values are the end result of careful, step-by-step logical reasoning, while contrary views and values derive from a mixture of prejudice, sentiment, mindless conformity, and wishful thinking. They ignore or minimize the inescapably subjective nature of the whole reasoning process. Highly intelligent people with the best possible motivations and logical skills start with the same objective data and end up with widely divergent and contradictory conclusions.[2] This does not render reason useless, but it should make rationalists more humble about their methodology than they often are.

Actually, even those of us most committed to logic and rationality do not so much reason our way to our views and values as _use_ reason to justify what we find ourselves believing and valuing. And those beliefs and values are likely to have been formed by our stories.[3] We tend not so much to use reason to construct our stories as to claim reasonableness for our stories after they have been formed. Stories shape us first, then reason is used, by those who feel it necessary, to lend credibility to the views and values that the often undetected stories have given us.

Why else are seemingly reasonable people so resistant to the evidence and reasoning of other reasonable people who hold different views? In our superficially rationalistic culture, it is usually unacceptable to say, "I believe this because it is the belief that has been passed on to me." We are supposed to have good _reasons_ for our beliefs. And so we sift around for the best reasons we can find to justify the positions we hold. But the underlying story is often more important than the logical supports we can muster for it. We will cling to our story long after reason has wandered off.

Story and reason, however, should not be seen as enemies. They are interwoven and complementary. We are drawn to story in part because we *are* rational and therefore desire the kind of order that story can provide. Or is it the other way around? Perhaps our reasoning abilities grow out of our story-tutored desire for connectedness. Either way, we should sacrifice neither story nor reason to the other.

Though we acknowledge their interdependence, it is still true that story gives us a kind of knowledge that abstract reasoning cannot. One of the advantages of *story knowledge* is its concreteness and specificity. Stories give us individualized people in specific times and places doing actual things. Rationality tends to sidestep the messy particulars to deal directly with the generalized concepts behind the particulars. In doing so it often strip-mines reality, washing away tons of seemingly useless details to get to the small golden nuggets of truth.

We certainly profit from the perception of generalized truths, but it is the conviction of story—and all art—that they can best be understood as they are embodied in the messy particulars. In the case of story, those are the particulars of time, person, place, and action. Story transfuses the pale abstractions of disembodied reason with the blood and bone of the senses and presents them for inspection by the whole person—rational, emotional, spiritual, sensual.

One area where this is most clearly seen is in ethical knowledge —the knowledge of how we are to behave. Our lives are an endless stream of choices, many of them having moral implications. How are we to *know* how to choose? Rationalism tells us to find universal principles that can, in theory, be applied to specific situations. But a problem arises. Equally rational people have been unable to agree, except at the most general and therefore least useful level, what those ethical principles are. The more general the principle, the more difficult to judge exactly how to apply it in any specific situation.

Looking to stories for genuine ethical knowledge is also not without difficulty. The very specificity of the story may make it seem too unique, obscuring its relation to my own ethical life. ("What has Hester Prynne's scarlet letter to do with me? I'm no hypocritical Puritan like her accusers.") But stories, much better than reason, do one thing that is essential to ethical behavior: they engage us wholly, including our emotions.

Consider the biblical story of the woman caught in adultery. The religious enemies of Jesus bring to him a woman caught in the act of adultery, an offense punishable by stoning according to the traditional law of Moses. They ask him whether she should be stoned, hoping to discredit him either as someone who rejects the moral law or as someone who sides against the common people.

As they are pressing him, Jesus bends down and writes something in the dirt. The rest of the story is as follows:

> When they persisted in questioning him, he stood and said, "Let the one who has no sin throw the first stone at her." Then he bent down again and wrote on the ground. After hearing this they began leaving one at a time, beginning with the oldest, until Jesus was left alone with the woman standing before him.
>
> He stood and said, "Woman, where are they? Has no one condemned you?"
>
> "No one, sir."
>
> "I do not condemn you either," Jesus said. "Go home and do not sin any more." (John 8)

Here is a treasure chest of ethical teaching in a brief story. We have characters, choices, actions, and meaning—all the elements of story. The story affirms the important truth that moral and immoral are valid categories and not just arbitrary names for personal opinions. That point was too obvious to need making in the first century, but is as necessary as it is controversial in our relativistic age. This story, like the overwhelming majority of stories, believes that good and evil genuinely exist and are knowable, and that the ability to distinguish between them is crucial to survival and to living well.

The story affirms not only that good and evil are real but that they are tied to human conduct. *We* can act in ways that are good and in ways that are evil. And it matters which we do.

Although this story rejects present-day moral relativism, it anticipates the modern emphasis on the frequent gap between appearances and reality, especially in questions of good and evil. The religious leaders who brought the woman to Jesus are ostensibly the good people of the community, those most concerned to do right. The story, of course, wishes us to see them as evil—interested not in right and wrong but only in destroying a religious rival, willing to sacrifice a real woman to make an abstract point.

We know immediately that the story wishes us to see them as villains, and we are glad to oblige with hisses. But honesty and the skill of the storyteller should also make us, if only briefly, identify with these religious leaders. We should be alerted to the many occasions in our own lives when we cover our base and selfish manipulations with high-sounding motivations, fooling ourselves more often than others.

We can also see ourselves in the place of the woman. We know what it is to be accused, to be caught red-handed, to have no excuses. (We can feel this even if we are so modern as not to believe adultery is evil.) We know what it is to need a break, to need to be treated better than we deserve.

And the story also invites us to put ourselves in the place of Jesus. We are invited to ask, "What would I do if I were in his shoes?" And then we are encouraged to consider what he in fact did. He saw through the hypocrisy of the questioners, he saw the humanity of the accused, and he saw the importance of acknowledging the validity of moral law.

His pointed answer to their question incorporates all the qualities of climax, surprise, and resolution that mark good stories: "Let the one among you who is guiltless throw the first stone." Here is an answer that is both dramatically and morally satisfying. The hypocrites are exposed, the humanity of the accused is affirmed, and the moral law is upheld, all in a way that was not quite imaginable only a moment before. What had seemed like an impossible dilemma was rendered a moment of the highest moral insight.

That insight is reinforced in the denouement of the story. As her accusers slink away, Jesus points out to the woman first her freedom and then her responsibility:

> He stood and said, "Woman, where are they? Has no one condemned you?"
>
> "No one, sir."
>
> "I do not condemn you either," Jesus said. "Go home and do not sin any more."

This story gives us knowledge—knowledge that is important, profound, and useful. It can help us live. This knowledge could not be conveyed with equal effectiveness by abstract reasoning, neither in these few words nor in many more. We *experience* the story, and experiences shape us in ways that abstractions cannot.[4]

Stanley Hauerwas and David Burrell claim that "story teaches us to know and do what is right under definite conditions" (16) and suggest further that "it seems unwise to separate a moral conviction from the story that forms its context of interpretation" (203n). Remove the "moral conviction" from the story that carries it and you risk removing its power to move us to apply it to our own story. They further observe that "we are given the impression that moral principles offer the actual ground for conduct, while in fact they present abstractions whose significance continues to depend on original narrative contexts" (26). Abstractions are useful, but that usefulness depends on the stories out of which they rise.

Why is story more powerful and therefore often more practical than abstract reasoning for imparting many kinds of knowledge? Because it appeals to all of what we are as human beings, not just to part of us. It recognizes that we are thinking, feeling, spiritual beings, with bodies that refuse to be ignored.

Story understands that if we do not know something emotionally we do not know it completely. That may be in part because, as

Martha Nussbaum argues, our emotions themselves are shaped by stories: "since one of the child's most pervasive and powerful ways of learning its society's values and structures is through the stories it hears and learns to tell, stories will be a major source of any culture's emotional life" (233–34).

But whatever the source of our emotions, story knows they must be treated with respect. It rejects the rationalistic prejudice that emotions get in the way of truth and knowledge, that they, along with other forms of subjectivity, must be suppressed if we are truly to know anything. Story says the opposite: If something ignores or rejects a crucial part of what I am, how can I know it to be true? This insistence on treating people wholly underlies D. H. Lawrence's immodest claim for storytellers: "being a novelist, I consider myself superior to the saint, the scientist, the philosopher, and the poet, who are all great masters of different bits of man alive, but never get the whole hog" (105).

I am mind, body, spirit—intertwined in such a way that nothing can happen to one without somehow affecting the other two. A merely sentimental story is not to be criticized because it appeals to the emotions, but because it appeals *only* to the emotions. An idea is limited not because it is cerebral, but only if it is solely cerebral, ignoring the rest of what we are.

This is why I think Smokey the Bear was more effective in getting a generation of Americans to worry about forest fires than are a labful of scientists in making us worry about global warming. Environmentalists need to find a story to give life to their message. Smokey the Bear derived from the story of a real bear cub found clinging in fright to a charred tree after a forest fire. Children could understand emotionally and intellectually the consequences of carelessness with fire in the forest. Throw in Bambi's problems with man-made forest fires and you have young apostles of fire prevention spreading the gospel throughout the land.

Contrast this with the reaction of many to environmentalists today. Environmentalists are bursting with facts, passion, and dire warnings. They may be more right than Smokey the Bear (contemporary theory being that forests are often best left to burn). But they have no story. They appeal to our intellects. They try, now and then, to shame and frighten us. Shame and fear are powerful but unsustainable emotions, and environmentalists have yet to touch the broader range of our emotions and thereby have failed to convince many to change their behavior. No matter how much our heads know, if our hearts are not persuaded, we are not truly convinced, certainly not enough to act.

In fact, there is more potential for creating a sense of caring gratitude and responsibility for the earth in Momaday's brief story about Devils Tower than in a library full of scholarly tomes. Tell us stories that make us feel connected to the universe around us and we will more likely take care of it. We need not so much more abstract knowledge about the environment as more story knowledge about our role in the natural world.

This is something the first Americans have understood better than those who came later. Consider the following passage from Momaday's *House Made of Dawn.* It is one of many extended descriptions of the natural surroundings within which the story takes place. It is wasted on many readers, who are anxious to get through such passages to places in the story where something *happens,* not understanding that knowing and accepting one's place in the created world is the most important *event* of all:

There is a kind of life that is peculiar to the land in summer—a wariness, a seasonal equation of well-being and alertness. Road runners take on the shape of motion itself, urgent and angular, or else they are like the gnarled, uncovered roots of ancient, stunted trees, some ordinary ruse of the land itself, immovable and forever there. And quail, at evening, just failing to suggest the waddle of too much weight, take cover with scarcely any talent for alarm, and spread their wings to the ground; and if then they are made to take flight, the imminence of no danger on earth can be more apparent; they explode away like a shot, and there is nothing but the dying whistle and streak of their going. Frequently in the sun there are pairs of white and russet

35

hawks soaring to the hunt. And when one falls off and alights, there will be a death in the land, for it has come down to place itself like a destiny between its prey and the burrow from which its prey has come; and then the other, the killer hawk, turns around in the sky and breaks its glide and dives. It is said that hawks, when they have nothing to fear in the open land, dance upon the warm carnage of their kills. In the highest heat of the day, rattlesnakes lie outstretched upon the dunes, as if the sun had wound them out and lain upon them like a line of fire, or, knowing of some vibrant presence on the air, they writhe away in the agony of time. And of their own accord they go at sundown into the earth, hopeless, as if to some unimaginable reckoning in the underworld. Coyotes have the gift of being seldom seen; they keep to the edge of vision and beyond, loping in and out of cover on the plains and highlands. And at night, when the whole world belongs to them, they parley at the river with the dogs, their higher, sharper voices full of authority and rebuke. They are an old council of clowns, and they are listened to. . . .

Great golden eagles nest among the highest outcrops of rock on the mountain peaks. They are sacred, and one of them, a huge female, old and burnished, is kept alive in a cage in the town. Even so, deprived of the sky, the eagle soars in man's imagination; there is divine malice in the wild eyes, an unmerciful intent. The eagle ranges far and wide over the land, farther than any other creature, and all things there are related simply by having existence in the perfect vision of a bird. (54–55)

The precise rightness of observations like "the quail, at evening, just failing to suggest the waddle of too much weight" provides more foundation for creating an instinct for preservation than a hundred hyperventilating reports on global carbon dioxide levels. Both science and stories seek knowledge through acute observation, but science is limited in making only *physical* connections between the things observed. This whole passage, on the other hand, senses with minute accuracy, feels with a wide range of emotion, and knows what can be done and what only marveled at. The knowledge that "all things . . . are related" can be approved by reason but is best felt and acted on through story. Such knowledge is a product less of analysis and deduction than of faith based on experience. Armed with such knowledge, we understand better how to save our world and ourselves.

Story provides us not only a way of knowing but also a way of remembering. Without memory, knowledge is useless. It floats around as disembodied bits of observation and assertion, impotent and homeless. Memory reminds us where any particular nugget of knowledge comes from, how it was discovered, how it has been used, where it has worked and where it hasn't. And the best medium for such memories is story. Stories preserve memories best because they give them a shape that attracts the mind.

Consider the following from a poem by Susan Griffin, "I Like to Think of Harriet Tubman":

> *I like to think of Harriet Tubman.*
> *Harriet Tubman who carried a revolver,*
> *who had a scar on her head from a rock thrown*
> *by a slave-master (because she*
> *talked back), and who*
> *had a ransom on her head*
> *of thousands of dollars and who*
> *was never caught, and who*
> *had no use for the law when the law was wrong,*
> *who defied the law. I like*
> *to think of her.*
> *I like to think of her especially*
> *when I think of the problem of*
> *feeding children. (263–65)*

Susan Griffin addresses a present, practical problem through memory and story. The specific problem is hungry children. A more general problem is the inadequacy of detached, abstract reasoning

37

(here associated with male politicians) to address a down-to-earth,
everyday reality:

> *The legal answer*
> *to the problem of feeding children*
> *is ten free lunches every month,*
> *being equal, in the child's real life,*
> *to eating lunch every other day.*

Larger still is the problem, treated in the rest of the poem, of how
men treat women and children.

Griffin *thinks* about these problems through the lens of Harriet
Tubman. Harriet Tubman was black and a woman and defied the
stereotypes associated with each category. She was strong, resourceful, persevering, intolerant of wrong, concerned for the well-being of
others, and, in case that wasn't enough, carried a gun.

When Susan Griffin thinks about the problem of hungry children, the example—the story—of Harriet Tubman informs her
thinking. It does not take the place of reason, but gives reason the
motivating force of passion and the particularity of historical fact.
Griffin, and her readers, understand their own responsibilities and
possibilities differently to the degree they make Harriet Tubman's
story—and now Griffin's—part of their own.

We all do what Griffin is doing here. We use memory of the past,
our personal and collective past, to help us think and feel our way
through the present. Remembering is the opposite of dismember-
ing. It is putting back together (re-member), or putting together for
the first time, fragmented parts of past experience in a way that
gives the past meaning for the present—and the result is story.

Memory in this sense is more than the ability to call something to
mind. It is *a stance toward* the person or event remembered, a
valuing of it, and a willingness to carry into the present what is good
and powerful from the past. It is conservative in the best sense of
the word, conserving the hard-won knowledge of often painful hu-

man experience, not to be frozen in sentimentality, but to be made new in the present.

Such a stance is inevitably a moral one. The Holocaust writer Theodor Adorno says, "Forgetting is inhuman because man's accumulated suffering is forgotten . . ." (quoted in Metz 95). Elie Wiesel sees his writing as an act of remembering with particular moral significance:

> But for me writing is a *matzeva,* an invisible tombstone, erected to the memory of the dead unburied. Each word corresponds to a face, a prayer, the one needing the other so as not to sink into oblivion. . . .
>
> Thus, the act of writing is for me often nothing more than the secret or conscious desire to carve words on a tombstone: to the memory of a town forever vanished, to the memory of a childhood in exile, to the memory of all those I loved and who, before I could tell them I loved them, went away. (25–26)

Remembering is a form of valuing, and what we choose to value and what to neglect is a measure of our morality. Societies that remember well and tell good stories are healthy societies. Those who use stories to kill time, compassion, and memory are doomed.

We have touched on just a few of the things that we know when we know a story. The novelist Reynolds Price offers a longer list:

> narrative, like the other basic needs of the species, supports the literal survival of man by providing him with numerous forms of nurture—the simple *companionship* of the narrative transaction, the *union* of teller and told; the narrator's opportunity for exercise of personal *skill* in telling and its ensuing rewards; the audience's exercise of *attention, imagination,* powers of *deduction;* the *spiritual support* which both parties receive from stories affirming our importance and protection in a perilous world; the transmission to younger listeners of *vital knowledge,* worldly or unworldly; the *narcotic effect* of narrative on pain and boredom; and perhaps most importantly, the chance that in the very attempt at narrative transaction *something new* will surface or be revealed, some sudden floater from the dark unconscious, some

message from a god which can only arrive or be told as a tale. (26; emphasis added)

Can we live without these things? We can certainly keep breathing. But I don't know that we can remain human. Take away stories and you take away our knowledge of how to live.

3

Characters Shaping Character: Beyond Personality

> . . . a man is always a teller of tales, he lives sur-
> rounded by his stories and the stories of others, he sees
> everything that happens to him through them; and he
> tries to live his life as if he were telling a story.
>
> Jean-Paul Sartre

We should worry less about our personality and more about our character. That we do the opposite is a testimony to the decline of a moral consensus and the current ascendancy of popular psychology over storytelling. We care too much about how we feel and how we are seen, and not enough about how we act and what we are. Seeing ourselves as characters in lifelong stories can help to correct this imbalance.

A fruitful but neglected link exists between the use of the term "character" in storytelling, on the one hand, and in ethics and personal development, on the other, that can supplement the too narrow understanding of the self offered by the social sciences. Our own characters are greatly shaped by the characters in the stories in which we partake, and we do well to use our knowledge of that influence to consider more consciously what kind of characters we are.

The single aspect of story that draws us most irresistibly is character. We remember characters from stories long after we've forgotten plot, language, and theme. I recall very few details of the *Iliad,* which I haven't read since high school, but I clearly remember Achilles sulking in his tent, Hector taking tender leave of his wife and child, and Cassandra raving the truth to people who didn't want to hear it. Most of the symbolism in *Moby Dick* has dropped into the same depths of the unconscious that store all the sermons I heard growing up, but I still quail with the others in the crew before Ahab, the archetypal obsessive.

The allure of character is the attraction of watching people make decisions. There have been many attempts to define what is unique about human beings in comparison with the animals. One crucial distinction has to do with the kind and quality of decisions we are required to make.

Our attraction to characters in stories is largely the same no matter what their source—literature, history, contemporary culture, family, or our own lives. In each case we are drawn to tales of fellow human beings facing choices that remind us of our own, or at the least prompt us to ask, "What would I do if . . . ?"

And in that question lies not only our humanity but also the potential for our own character to be formed by the characters in our stories. For while that question—"What would I do?"—hangs in the air, who we are is up for grabs. Answering the question does not simply entail *discovering* who we are but allows us in part to *determine* who we are. Every powerful character we encounter in story is a challenge to our own character, and holds the possibility of changing us.

In Chapter 1, I defined character as a bundle of values in action. Wayne Booth argues that character is whatever *persists* in an individual, the habits of choice that shape who we essentially are even as what is not essential about us is in a constant process of change and, eventually, decay (8).[1] Character is who and what you are in your essence, after much that is transient and superficial is stripped away. It includes both your inner and outer life, but is best revealed in the many things you do—especially in those little things that you do without thinking too much.

Consider Huck Finn. In _Adventures of Huckleberry Finn,_ Mark Twain gives a character the greatest freedom that anyone can give to another—the freedom to tell his or her own story. Allowing Huck to tell his own story in his own words is the key to the power of the novel and the immortality of the character.

The process of character formation is, in fact, the central preoccupation of the story. Huck Finn is, in the timeless pattern of so many stories, adolescent innocence coming to terms with adult experience. He is faced with innumerable choices, many of them microcosms of the devastating choices facing the nation at that time, or facing human beings at any time.

How he responds to each choice is a reflection of his character in the literary and ethical as well as developmental senses. As he analyzes, agonizes, theorizes, and rationalizes, we get an insight both into who he already is and into what he is becoming. An early struggle over the ethics of stealing food while on the run is typical:

Mornings, before daylight, I slipped into corn fields and borrowed a watermelon, or a mushmelon, or a punkin, or some new corn, or things of that kind. Pap always said it warn't no harm to borrow things, if you was meaning to pay them back, sometime; but the widow said it warn't anything but a soft name for stealing, and no decent body would do it. Jim said he reckoned the widow was partly right and pap was partly right; so the best way would be for us to pick out two or three things from the list and say we wouldn't borrow them any more—then he reckoned it wouldn't be no harm to borrow the others. So we talked it over all one night, drifting along down the river, trying to make up our minds whether to drop the watermelons, or the cantelopes, or the mushmelons, or what. But towards daylight we got it all settled satisfactory, and concluded to drop crabapples and p'simmons. We warn't feeling just right, before that, but it was all comfortable now. I was glad the way it come out, too, because crabapples ain't ever good, and the p'simmons wouldn't be ripe for two or three months yet. (56; ch. 12)

Our laughter at Huck's self-deceptive rationalizing does not prevent us from seeing his essential morality. He is trying hard to be a good person. If he doesn't quite measure up to the external standards for such a person, that gives us more comfort than concern, because we are all too aware of our own difficulty in keeping the letter of the law.

There are more important things at stake in *Huckleberry Finn,* however, than watermelons and crabapples. At the center of the novel is the relationship between Huck and the runaway slave, Jim. Huck is a boy of his time (pre-Civil War America) struggling to break free of the inhumanity of that time—and all times. And it *is* a struggle. If it weren't, the story would not interest us.

Huck constantly rehearses what he knows he is supposed to do, as taught to him by society, and what he feels he ought to do, as he is learning from his personal experience with Jim. He comes down alternately on one side and then on the other. What finally tilts him in the right direction (and Twain and the reader both are sure there is a *right* direction) is his entanglement in the story of Jim's life.

The abstract law says Jim is a runaway slave and must be returned. Only Huck's growing awareness of Jim's humanity and pain allows Huck to question that public morality (think again of Christ and the woman caught in adultery). He must move from seeing Jim as a stereotype (a move Twain himself did not entirely achieve) to seeing him as an individual human being with a story:

> I went to sleep, and Jim didn't call me when it was my turn. He often done that. When I waked up, just at day-break, he was setting there with his head down betwixt his knees, moaning and mourning to himself. I didn't take notice, nor let on. I knowed what it was about. He was thinking about his wife and his children, away up yonder, and he was low and homesick; because he hadn't ever been away from home before in his life; and I do believe he cared just as much for his people as white

folks does for their'n. It don't seem natural, but I reckon it's so. He was often moaning and mourning that way, nights, when he judged I was asleep, and saying, "Po' little 'Lizabeth! po' little Johnny! its mighty hard; I spec' I ain't ever gwyne to see you no mo', no mo'!" He was a mighty good nigger, Jim was. (125; ch. 23)

Yes, Jim is still "nigger" to Huck, a fact that has led some of late to reject *Huckleberry Finn* as a racist novel. But if Huck's (and Twain's) moral education is not complete, might that not raise in our minds the salutary thought that neither is our own? Which of us so perfectly lives up to our moral vision that we can eagerly reach for the first stone? If Huck and Twain are alternately morally sensitive and morally obtuse, so are we all, and an awareness of that condition is one of the healthy outcomes possible from our encounter with characters like Huck and Jim.

The extended ripples from a story like this were recently reinforced for me. During a rare visit to my hometown, I looked up a friend I hadn't seen in many years. I was pleasantly surprised to be greeted at the front door by a young white-haired boy, and delighted to learn that his name is Huckleberry. In my unparalleled discretion, I raised no eyebrows, and asked no questions. But his father offered a whiff of an explanation anyway: "I always liked the novel . . . and the values."

Naming his boy Huckleberry signaled my friend's implicit recognition that there is some connection between the characters in our stories and the person we want to be. Most societies have believed in the importance of naming. Your name is your destiny. You are linked to someone in the past—from history, family, religion—in the hope that the character of that earlier person would somehow be linked to your own. I believe my friend named his son Huckleberry not because it went particularly well with Rheinschmidt (his last name), but because he wanted some part of his son to be like Huck.

And all of us want to be something like the characters in the stories we value. Bruno Bettelheim suggests that the tendency of major characters in fairy tales to be either wholly good or wholly evil, while not realistic, is necessary to their effectiveness in nurturing the child's moral development: "Then the child has a basis for understanding that there are great differences between people, and that therefore one has to make choices about who one wants to be. This basic decision, on which all later personality development will build, is facilitated by the polarizations of the fairy tale" (9).

Bettelheim follows this with an intriguing assertion: "The question for the child is not 'Do I want to be good?' but 'Who do I want to be like?'" (10). Philosophy and some other disciplines make it their business to investigate the question "What is meant by the concept 'good'?" But only story can deal with the question "Who do I want to be like?" I would argue that the latter is a much more important question, not least because the answer determines the shape of human experience.

It is not surprising that the bulk of moral education in human history has been through models, exempla, heroes—that is, through story. Many of the traditional stories of moral education have fallen out of favor because of modern skepticism, the loss of centers of moral authority, fear of hypocrisy, and suspicion that morality might be just another name for authoritarianism, privilege, and power.

We don't even like the word "morality" anymore. We are afraid someone we don't respect is going to use it in a way that makes the world worse instead of better. Literary scholars, those who make their living off responding to stories, have until recently been more insistent than anyone else that story and morality, aesthetics and ethics, be kept safely removed from each other.

Fortunately it is not possible. Characters and stories center on choices, and where there is a question of alternatives, there is always the question of values *(why* choose this over that)—hence, of morality. That pronouncements of good and evil, right and wrong have been abused should not prevent us from seeing that our life choices have inescapable moral dimensions and that stories play a crucial role.

My friend is not the only one whose way of thinking was influenced by Huck Finn. Robert Coles discusses the impact of the novel on one of his patients, a boy named Phil. Phil had contracted polio (which would eventually lead to the amputation of both legs), both his parents were dead, and not surprisingly he was, to use his own word, "moody."

As a young psychiatrist, Coles was supposed to help Phil. His best clinical approaches were met with skepticism. Only when they started talking about stories was progress made. At the prodding of a teacher who visited him in the hospital, Phil reread *Huckleberry Finn*. It gave him a new resource for thinking about his life and what had befallen him. Confined now to a bed for the rest of his life, he found that prospect less despairing because of a story:

> "I can't explain what happened; I know that my mind changed after I read *Huckleberry Finn*. I couldn't get my mind off the book. I forgot about myself—no, I didn't, actually. I joined up with Huck and Jim; we became a trio. They were very nice to me. I explored the Mississippi with them on the boats and on the land. I had some good talks with them. I dreamed about them. I'd wake up, and I'd know I'd just been out west, on the Mississippi. I talked with those guys, and they straightened me out!" (35–36)

As Phil learned, you do not lose yourself in the best stories. Rather you find yourself—or at least a potential self. You don't ultimately *become* the character in the story, though you may for a time; you *join with* that character, discovering not only what he or she can do, but what the two of you can do together. Phil later added Holden Caulfield to the group, and who knows what other characters. They became part of his mental and spiritual universe. They quite literally became part of who he was. (The same identification can happen with evil or vacuous characters. If stories have any power at all, they have the power to harm as well as to help.)

As I indicated in Chapter 1, I had an experience similar to Phil's at a comparable age. Sometime in late adolescence I read J. R. R.

47

Tolkien's *The Lord of the Rings*. I was drawn not so much to the plot of the adventure as to the characters having the adventure. Maybe it is better to say that the testing of their character *was* the adventure for me—as I later realized it was for Tolkien as well.

The story gave me courage to say to myself what I already felt to be true from my own experience—that good and evil are real, that it mattered a great deal which one wins out in the world, and that the outcome depended on me. *The Lord of the Rings* is filled with unexceptional people—that is, hobbits, elves, and the like—called on to do exceptional things if good is going to survive in the world. Like Phil in reading *Huckleberry Finn*, I discovered that I did not so much forget myself as find myself going along on the adventure, dealing like the nonheroic, comfort-loving hobbits with weariness, fear, uncertainty, and agonizing choices. With them I felt terror when confronted with undisguised evil and enormous gratefulness for unexpected good.

Reading *The Lord of the Rings* (and its predecessor, *The Hobbit*) reinforced in me a tremendous desire that good should win in the world and evil be defeated, and to do what I could to help—not least because the story helped me see that evil was not only out there, but within me as well. I believe this story helped shape who I was and am. Its characters became a part of my character. The literary, ethical, and psychosocial notions of character were all at work in this one experience with story.

After reading *The Lord of the Rings* two or three times in my teens, I have not read it since. I might not be nearly so impressed now, but that doesn't matter. It did me a service. It helped form my mind as well as my ethics at a time when both were up for grabs. When I later discovered sophistic thinkers who assured me that good and evil were not real categories but only subjective and transient points of view, I knew better. I lacked then the intellectual resources to articulate my disagreement, but I was armed with the holistic experience of a story that kept me from naively embracing what I now think is a widely influential but unlivable view of the world.[2]

Lest you think this is merely a phenomenon of overly impression-
able adolescents, think about the characters in your own life. Who
are the characters from your past or present who, like it or not, are
in some way part of your character? What grandparent, teacher,
parent, friend, enemy, brother or sister? What writer, musician,
entertainer? What politician, social reformer, thinker? What saint,
martyr, or holy fool?

Reynolds Price tells such a story from his own family: "My father
was seriously alcoholic in the six years of marriage before my birth;
when both my mother and I were endangered in a difficult labor, he
made a vow to quit his drinking if both of us lived; we did and he
quit. I was told of the vow by the time I was five and from then on
saw myself in stronger light as a pledge, a hostage with more than
normal duties and perils" (13). By changing his image of himself at
an early age, that story altered who he was and what his place was to
be in the world.

I have written elsewhere of a dying woman named Phyllis (23).
She was the divorced wife of my father's friend from college days, in
her fifties, and dying of cancer. She seemed to have little to show for
her life. Her marriage had dissolved long ago, she had traveled paths
her well-known preacher father would never have approved, her
beloved daughter had been killed in a car wreck a few years before,
and she was broke.

As college students, my wife-to-be and I visited her in her last
days. The room was bare and dingy, the walls painted a dirty-looking
tan. She sat in the reclining chair in which she slept because it was
too painful for her to lie down. A curly wig covered her baldness.
Nothing in the situation hinted at the greatness of spirit that filled
the woman.

She talked to us about life in the way that only those with little of
it left can do. All the trivial urgencies of daily living had seeped
away. Nothing petty was worth her attention—or, for those moments, ours. She talked, among other things, about her pain, but in
a way I had never heard anyone talk. She addressed it as her companion, as her escort to another world. She said God sometimes

came to her in the night, a warm light that filled her body and assured her that all shall be well. Our culture's great aversion to pain and suffering of any kind was, she thought, a bad sign. Pain was a part of so many good things—giving birth, writing a poem, asking forgiveness, even saying I love you. Complete freedom from pain meant separation from life.

After being with Phyllis, I could never think of pain, my own or the world's, in quite the same way. She gave me a fresh way of seeing something that was very old and familiar. She did not erase the reality of suffering but she offered me new ways of thinking about it. And therefore I have evaluated and acted in the world slightly differently in the many years since. I have been, in short, a different character, and thereby lived a slightly different story, because of this brief encounter with a dying woman whose life had all the external marks of failure.

But why use this special vocabulary of character and story here? Everyone knows that other people are important in our lives and influence us. How does calling this woman a "character" help us see anything more clearly than simply referring to her as an important person in my life? Because the concepts of character and story highlight the aspect of *experience and choices over time* that makes each of us what we are and that is at the heart of the definition of story. My experience with Phyllis had the impact it did only because it represented the coming briefly together of two stories, not simply two persons. Phyllis had a history, including experience with great physical, psychological, and spiritual pain, that *made* her what she was, and only that history gave her the possibility of being an influence on others.

Furthermore, she could not and did not influence my personality —that had long since been set—but she could affect my character, the me who is an actor, chooser, thinker, doer in my own story. Only because she had been shaped by her story could she shape mine. The concepts of story and character strike me not only as appropriate for describing who we are and our interactions together but as greatly superior to many other kinds of terminology now being used, including that of traditional psychotherapy, the current monopolizer of all talk about human beings.

One indication of our society's malaise in the last few generations is the replacement of the concept of *character* in popular culture with that of *personality*. We are obsessed with our personalities but neglectful of our characters. The bookstores and talk shows are crammed with personality-speak: finding yourself, accepting yourself, loving yourself, fulfilling yourself, developing yourself, esteeming yourself, asserting yourself, changing yourself, healing yourself, and so on. All of this revolves around a conception of the self formed largely by psychology.

And psychology does not like to talk about character. It is too messy, too imprecise, too unmeasurable—that is, too human. The banishment of character from psychology was complete well before mid-century. Gordon Allport, an eminent Harvard psychologist and onetime president of the American Psychological Association, expressed the still common view when he wrote in the 1930s that we should "admit frankly that [character] is an ethical concept" and that, as such, "the psychologist does not need the term at all; personality alone will serve" (*Personality* 52).

Psychology is happier to talk about personality than character because the latter is too value-laden, as Allport himself makes clear: "*Character is personality evaluated, and personality is character devaluated.*" Psychology took the ancient idea of character, an idea that was central to education and moral development, stripped out value judgments (especially assessments of right and wrong), and gave us personality to take its place. Or, to use Allport's own terms, the notion of moral excellence (character) was replaced by that of social and personal effectiveness (personality). Defining the self by character traits like courage, honesty, and loyalty gave way to definition by personality traits like assertiveness, self-confidence, and compulsiveness.

Psychology felt it had to eliminate character because it wanted to be a science, and science was supposed to be objective.[3] Story embraces character because it never wants to be objective. Story, like all art, is rooted in the personal, subjective, concrete, historical.

Look again at Allport's definition of personality as "character devaluated." Likely he meant the self looked at objectively, unencumbered by controversial and imprecise values—"ethical moss" he calls them (*Pattern* 32)—but I would argue that the net effect of the replacement in popular culture of the language of character by that of personality (and that replacement is almost total) has been the literal devaluing—valuing less—of human beings and the human experience. This is not the fault of psychology per se, which has the right to limit what it investigates, but of the wholesale adoption of this way of understanding the human person by a naive and confused society. Psychology, as Allport claims, may not need the concept of character, but human beings and human society do.

Psychology, of course, has long made a use of story. Classic psychoanalysis encouraged a fragmented storytelling in its dream analysis and exploration of childhood experiences. Jung explored and celebrated and sought to use stories from many cultures. But Freud was more interested in the fragments of a person's story as a clue to the unconscious than he was in the conscious choices that a person made or in the place that person had in the story of the larger community. And Jung has been more influential on art and literature than on contemporary psychotherapy.

With a few exceptions, modern psychotherapy has followed in the footsteps of its founders and early practitioners in preferring to approach human nature individualistically through the seemingly value-neutral avenue of personality, rather than by the value-laden road of character. It has emphasized inner states of being over external behaviors—traits and habits over choices with ethical implications. Though the advantages of this approach are apparent, there is also a loss. To the degree that any approach to the human experience ignores life's constant demand that we make choices rooted in values, it diminishes our humanity and reduces its own relevance to daily living.

Story can rescue us from this overly narrow conception of who we are, especially as expressed in popular culture. We need not displace psychology and the concept of personality, but we desperately need to supplement that concept with the more holistic understanding that story and character provide. Character is values lived. It is more nearly what we genuinely are than anything contained in dozens of psychological categories and descriptions. You define yourself by your choices, your daily actions in the real world. These choices, of course, will be influenced by temperament and traits and inner states of being, but these things neither define nor determine you. Your character remains after all those labels have been exhausted. It is that unique stamp that both unites us with and separates us from every other human being ever born. It probes at what cannot be successfully measured or charted. It is therefore imprecise, subjective, and unscientific. It exudes values, particularity, choices, regrets, hopes, dilemmas, unpredictability, and on and on.[4]

The perfect net to hold all this humanness is story. And it is through exposure to the characters in story that our own character is most likely to be molded. Because stories engage so much of who we are—our rationality, emotions, imaginations, spirituality, and even our bodies—the characters in them have an unparalleled power to move us. These characters may come from literature, family, history, popular culture, or our own lives, but it is our witnessing of their entanglement in their own stories that enables us to identify with them and allow them into our own.

There are many advantages to having our character, and the values that inform our character, consciously formed by story rather than by other means. Story subverts our instinctive distaste for abstract rules. Codes smell of failure. They make clear to our intellects what we have failed to live in our lives. Even if they express concepts with which we wholly agree, and to which we aspire, their very existence whispers that we are unlikely to achieve them.

Story gets around this by making believable and attractive a kind of *life* that we can imagine ourselves living. What is abstract and off-putting in codified, rationalistic form—literally *unrealistic*—is irresistible and compelling in story form because we enter into that story world and are changed in it as whole persons.[5] The admonition to respect people of other races, for instance, is insipid compared to the impact of floating with Huck and Jim down the Mississippi. The most effective long-term solution to racism, as to many other ills, is generations of exchanged and interwoven stories.

Stories, of course, do not exist to "illustrate" or make palatable ethical or philosophical truths. Good stories defy any reduction to a moral or bit of wisdom. The *particular* values and wisdom of a story do not even exist prior to or apart from the story. Whatever is in the story is paradoxically so unique that it exists only in the actions of these characters making these choices at this time, and, at the same time, partakes of something universal and generalizable enough to touch me and my time. Story acts by incarnation, giving flesh and life to what otherwise is detached and abstract.

Only because story catches the universal and abstract in the net of particulars can it shape what we do in the world. We saw earlier that "story teaches us to know and do what is right *under definite conditions*" (Hauerwas and Burrell 16; emphasis added). This view rejects the prevalent idea that rational objectivity is the key to ethical analysis and development: "Any ethical theory that is sufficiently abstract and universal to claim neutrality would not be able to form character. For it would have deprived itself of the notions and convictions which are the necessary conditions for character. Far from assuring truthfulness, a species of rationality which prizes objectivity to the neglect of particular stories distorts moral reasoning by the way it omits the stories of character formation. If truthfulness (and the selflessness characteristic of moral behavior) is to be found, it will have to occur in and through the stories that tie the contingencies of our life together" (24).

When I am tempted, as I always am, to put my personal advantage ahead of the common good—in my home or in society—I am little moved by abstract ethical injunctions, and actively encouraged to "me-firstism" by psychological-sounding appeals to my needs and rights. But I can sometimes be nudged toward something resembling concern for others by remembering a story from long ago about wizards and hobbits.

Further, stories are not only human, they are humane—even those filled with inhumane characters. Stories ask for understanding. They encourage us to see the complexity of the simplest choices, to understand the forces that, if they do not rob us of our freedom, at least so buffet that freedom as to encourage us sometimes to do what we hate. Stories tend to make us more tolerant and forgiving of moral failure at the same time that they convince us of the reality and necessity of the moral dimension of life. A person steeped in stories is less likely to be judgmental, but more likely to realize that judgments must be made.

It is helpful to consciously identify and choose among the characters in the stories that surround us, because as characters in our own story, we are creating ourselves by the choices we make. The quality of our own lives is directly related to the quality of the stories in which we participate. Huck, Phyllis, Pascal, Alyosha Karamazov, a half dozen teachers in my life, Martin Luther King, Jr., a hobbit or two, and many, many others are among the characters in stories—historical, fictional, and familial—that have drawn me into their stories and by so doing made my story and my character what it is.

If our character depends to a significant degree on the stories in which we participate, how important it is that they be good ones. Most of us can rise no higher than the level of the stories that surround us. Some transcend their broken stories, though only by finding a new story to guide them.

What is a _good_ story? Pragmatic, experiential answers are better than abstract ones. A good story is one that makes _you_ good, or at least better. I mean this in the widest sense. Good stories don't simply make you a nicer or more ethical person—though some can; they draw out of you more of what makes you a feeling, giving, thinking, creating, laughing, curious human being. This is not the necessary result of every individual story—stories are valuable on other scores—but it should be the cumulative effect of your stories collectively.

The point is not to forbid bad stories, but to instill a hunger for good ones. If popular culture offers us primarily trivial stories peopled with cardboard characters that appeal to what is least significant in us, then we must turn elsewhere for our stories. Fortunately they are all around—if only we have the eyes to see and the ears to hear. These stories lie waiting in our families, in world literature, in history, in the communities of which we are a part, in our places of worship—in our hearts.

Long after the latest therapy fad and its trendy catchphrases are forgotten, people will still be telling stories and finding that the stories change their lives. The best road to a healthy self lies in the question "Who do I want to be like?" In answering that character question—not in fine-tuning our personalities—we create ourselves. And our greatest resource is story.

4

Finding a Plot in Our Lives: The Search for Meaning and a Happy Ending

Accident without significance is boring.
                                        John Gardner

[Myth] tends like prophecy to shape a future to
confirm it.
                                        Frank Kermode

Who can deny that things to come are not yet? Yet
already there is in the mind an expectation of things
to come.
                                        Augustine

After air, food, and water, the thing we most need is that our lives
mean something. That life is meaningless, arbitrary, and random is
espoused in many places, believed in few, and accepted with equa-
nimity in none. The desperate eloquence of many who insist that
such is the nature of life is itself a testimony to our passionate desire
for meaning. We complain most bitterly about the lack of that which
we most need. But in articulating our fear that there is no meaning
—as we often do in art or literature or religion—we bear ironic

57

witness to an underlying order which our disappointment with life sometimes causes us to deny.

Story is a vessel for carrying meaning. Meaning inhabits story the way a morning mist envelops a pine forest—everywhere present, but nowhere tangible. Detach meaning from story and both die.

So it is with our lives. Nothing makes us want to live more than the feeling that we have something important to do. Nothing makes life seem as worthless as the feeling that we do not. Seeing our lives as a story interacting with other stories gives us that sense of being part of a sequence of meaningful events that lead to a significant conclusion. In short, one criterion for meaning is that we find a plot in our lives.

Many locate the origin of narrative and plot in the very beginnings of human experience. Northrup Frye suggests that the first rituals—and therefore the first steps toward art and religion—arose out of an awareness of repetition in nature (682). The daily alternation of day and night, sun and moon; the coming and going and coming again of the seasons; the appearance, disappearance, and then reappearance of migrating animals; even that steady beating in the chest suggested that pattern, rhythm, sequence were at the core of life.

The ability to recognize these patterns, and to pattern one's own actions after them, increased the odds of surviving. It still does. We live better and longer if we can find a pattern, a plot, to our lives. MacIntyre claims that when someone complains that their life is meaningless, they often are really saying that "the narrative [story] of their life has become unintelligible to them, that it lacks any point, any movement towards a climax or a telos" (217). We need the sense of a coherent story to our lives, a significant connection between its major episodes, and the reasonable hope that it will have a satisfactory conclusion.

If we have this sense that our lives have a meaningful plot, we can absorb every kind of tragedy and suffering without despair. If we do not have this sense, no amount of good news is good enough. Story gives us a context for coming to terms with that which is otherwise unbearable. It allows us to name and reconcile with that which otherwise presents itself to us as misery, horror, absurdity, or chaos.

I will illustrate with a story about a photograph. I have created for myself a story about this photograph, one that may or may not have been true for those in the picture. It is a grainy black-and-white photograph taken from below at some distance from its subjects—a man and a boy, and a soldier with a gun. To the side of them are people standing in line, and, perhaps, dead bodies. The place is somewhere in Eastern Europe—Poland, I think. And the time, of course, is Holocaust time, the time when all stories, all coherence, are most called into question.

As I remember it—my mind may have added this detail—the man had on the flat-brimmed hat and wore the side curls of the Hasidim, those most fervent and pious and joyous of Jews. The boy beside him was quite small—five, maybe six years old. It was their turn to die.

How did this man spend his last moments? He spent them telling a story, or at least it seems so to me. Because at the moment the photographer snapped the shutter—and who was that photographer?—the man in the hat was bending down to the face of the boy and at the same time pointing his finger up to the sky. I believe he was telling him a story and I imagine that the story went something like this: "Do not be afraid, my son. This man cannot really hurt us. He is going to send us to heaven where we will join your mother and sister. God is waiting for us. Everything is going to be all right."

The man, I believe, was making use of the story he had embraced for his life to come to terms with his and his son's horrific end. I choose to see it as an act of defiance. Deprived of all other means of resistance, he resists the man with the rifle and all that man represents in the most powerful way of all—he insists on the superiority and ultimate triumph of his own story. "You, killer, think you have the gun and I am nothing. But I, killer, have God and you have nothing." The man, however, does not actually say this to his executioner, or likely even think it. He has something infinitely more important to do. He has to comfort for a few moments longer a frightened child. And he does so by interpreting this final, terrifying event in light of the story of their whole lives.

I am filled with ambivalence about my reading of that photograph. Not so much about whether my understanding is correct as about having put it down in writing for others to see. Some will be outraged, in principle, by any attempt to find silver linings in the unqualified abomination that is the Holocaust. Others will see it as a sin against those pictured, putting words of hope into the mouth of a man who might well have been cursing the very God I imagine him invoking. Still others will claim, not incorrectly, that my story of the photograph tells us nothing about those pictured, but only reveals my own need to be comforted.

In fact, I do not even know if I am remembering the picture accurately, having seen it years ago in a book I can no longer find. But it doesn't matter. Their story, as I imagine it, is now part of my own story. The courage and faith I ascribe to them make it more possible for me to believe that courage and faith are realistic options for me under infinitely less oppressive circumstances. If others choose to read that photograph differently, then they will use it in their own stories as they see fit.

Aristotle long ago announced that stories have beginnings, middles, and ends. That didn't seem very helpful to me the first time I heard it. It does now. Many spend a fair amount of time in the long middles of their lives thinking about what happened before and what will come after. By connecting those three aspects of story time—past, present, and future—we hope to devise a plot for our lives that will give significance to the whole.

Let us think for a moment about beginnings, middles, and ends. Beginnings do not begin unless they lead to something. We cannot even use the word "beginning" without implying something connected to that beginning and growing out of it. Language insists on connectedness even when the harassed reason wants to say it isn't so.

So does biology. No living thing is static (and even rock formations change over time). Everywhere we look we see development, change, movement from stage to stage. Potential becomes actual, implicit explicit, foreshadowed realized. If this is only one way of seeing the world, it is the dominant one for our time and one that, now having seen it this way, we can never entirely abandon.

And this is also the way we look at the beginnings of our own stories. The Romantic poet Wordsworth nudged us in this direction two hundred years ago when he claimed, "The Child is father of the Man." One writer argues that the beginning of any story of fiction should contain "a compressed emotional promise of things to come" (Boles 8). With Wordsworth (and Freud) we search our murky beginnings for clues that explain what we have become today. We are convinced the two are related, and that conviction is undergirded by the influence of plot and story.

The beginnings of stories, our own and others', establish the setting and introduce the first characters. Such beginnings are full of promises—the promise of people we will come to care about, of significant action (things done that are worth doing), of curiosity aroused and eventually satisfied. Story's most basic promise is that it will not waste our time. We will not come to the end of it and say, "I could have spent my time better mowing the lawn."

Not every story keeps its promises. Some fail to make us care about their characters. Others fail to convince us that anything worthwhile is happening. Some debase our healthy human curiosity by making us detached voyeurs. Still others abuse the language of storytelling with cliché, sentimentality, or pretentiousness. All in all, failed stories leave us feeling we have wasted part of our lives.

Now, more than ever, we need faith in the promise of beginnings. If modern psychology has been helpful in drawing us to the beginnings of our stories to find clues to our present, it has distorted that search by its obsession with failure. Since its inception, psychotherapy has overwhelmingly focused on what is wrong with our stories rather than what is right with them. It has replaced the puritanical nose for sin with the psychiatric nose for abuse and discord.

Everyone looking back on the beginnings of his or her story is expected to find pain, distortion, and abuse or be accused of repression or dishonesty. As old-time religion encouraged us to ferret out sin everywhere, so we could confess and be absolved of it, so modern social science encourages us everywhere to find oppression, deformity, perversion, and misused power. This narrowness encourages us to undervalue our own beginnings and to see ourselves as helpless victims with damaged personalities rather than as active characters with the power to shape our own plots.

I could create a story of my own childhood that focuses on trouble and pain. The many individual details would be true but the story would be a lie. As with many people, troubling things were part of my beginnings, but none of them set the tone, none of them tell the story.

Although it's embarrassing to admit, I had a happy childhood. None of the many problems kept me from feeling loved and therefore secure. None of the imperfections, in my parents or in me or in the twenty or so homes in which we lived or in Truman-Eisenhower-Kennedy-Johnson America, made me into a doomed, tragic figure. I grew up, naively perhaps, thinking I had a reasonable chance to put together a successful life, and that the future, not the past, would determine the issue.

The point is not to tell only Pollyanna tales about one's beginnings. It is to see tales of pain in the context of a larger whole. We should marvel as much that pain coexists with and even stimulates good as we lament pain's destructive consequences. We ought not to allow our current obsession with finding something to blame for our discontent blind us to the life-enhancing possibilities that flicker in even the darkest stories. If we do, the beginning of our story will be of little help to us as we contemplate its middle and end.

The middle is the longest and most telling part of our life's story. We start thinking we are in the middle of our lives in adolescence, and continue thinking that way until near the end. Life's middle

requires of us almost endless choices, each with its attendant consequences, leading then to further choices. It is easy to think of our
lives as complicated plots, but hard to see that we have much
control over them or knowledge of where they are going.

When diagramming fictional stories, we speak of the middle as
the time of complication. All the potential conflicts that are incipient in the givens of beginning make themselves felt. These include
the givens of race, gender, class, and genetics, but also of setting,
situation, and historical moment, of family, personality, religion,
and so on.

For Huck Finn those latent conflicts include the existence of the
dehumanizing institution of slavery and his own relation to it. In the
beginning he can live as though the existence of slavery requires no
particular response from him. He did not invent it; he does not
practice it; he does not have the power to end it.

Or does he?

Huck's story changes forever when it gets mixed up with Jim's
story. Huck the adolescent can never again be Huck the child.
Whether by mere accident or larger design (is anything in a _story_
ever really an accident?), Huck encounters Jim, the runaway slave.
All Huck has ever wanted is to be free—of the Widow Douglas's
insistent do-gooding, of Pap's elemental harshness. Now he is confronted with another man who wants to be free, and whose freedom
depends on him.

Huck doesn't want the job. Life has been fishing, caving, explor-
ing wrecks, staying clear of obligations. He would like to stay with
his beginnings, but it is the inescapable nature of reality to move
from beginnings to middles, from simplicity to complication, from
innocence to experience. Because his story has intersected Jim's, he
must now make choices. He must now take on the conscious role of
a character in his own story.

And so must we. As we move from the innocence of beginnings
to the complication of middles, we are confronted with choices,
some of which we would rather not make. Many forces in modern
thought whisper to us that in fact we do not actually have any

choices at all. For all our individualism, we seem to have a fear and loathing of true freedom. Growing from the deterministic seeds embedded in Darwin, Marx, and Freud, and egged on by the radical skepticism of postmodernism in the humanities, the view has spread that we are powerless to shape the character of our own lives. Instead, all but the most trivial issues of life are decided for us by some combination of genetic inheritance, evolutionary selection, social conditioning, unconscious psychological forces, gender, class, or race.

Stories tell us otherwise. They insist on the link between character and plot. "What is character," Henry James asked, "but the determination of incident? What is incident but the illustration of character?" (13). Everything that *happens* in a story has the potential for revealing and forming character. The essence of plot is characters choosing. Like it or not, story tells us we are free and therefore responsible. We may be failures but we are not robots.

Are we really free? The question does not lend itself to proof. But our lives present themselves to us as though we are. All the arguments that we are not really free do not save us from the endless stream of choices that flows our way. Seeing our lives as meaningful stories with a significant plot encourages us to act on that perception of freedom—and thereby makes our stories and our world different.

As it did for Huck Finn. Huck finds he does, in fact, have the power to end slavery—at least in his own life and relationships. He can reject the arguments of slavery, expose their illusory foundations in dehumanization, and purpose to be different—even if it means he will go to hell.

Of course Huck does not use the artificial language or reasoning of academics—dehumanization, power, and so on. He is moved not by abstract logic but by Jim's story and specific memories of their shared story together. Having written a letter to Jim's owner informing her of Jim's whereabouts, his initial feeling of having done the right thing gives way under the pressure of shared experience:

I felt good and all washed clean of sin for the first time I had ever felt so in my life, and I knowed I could pray now. But I didn't do it straight off, but laid the paper down and set there thinking—thinking how good it was all this happened so, and how near I come to being lost and going to hell. And went on thinking. And got to thinking over our trip down the river; and I see Jim before me, all the time, in the day, and in the night-time, sometimes moonlight, sometimes storms, and we a floating along, talking, and singing, and laughing. (169; ch. 31)

Huck engages in moral reasoning, "set thinking," to reassure himself that turning Jim in is the right thing. But he "went on thinking," literally thinks again, in a way that undermines his previous judgment. And that thinking is story thinking: "I see Jim before me . . ." And the Jim he sees is the Jim with whom he has a relationship and shared experiences that cannot be left out of his moral reasoning:

But somehow I couldn't seem to strike no places to harden me against him, but only the other kind. I'd see him standing my watch on top of his'n, stead of calling me, so I could go on sleeping; and see him how glad he was when I come back out of the fog; and when I come to him again in the swamp, up there where the feud was; and such-like times; and would always call me honey, and pet me, and do everything he could think of for me, and how good he always was; and at last I struck the time I saved him by telling the men we had small-pox aboard, and he was so grateful, and said I was the best friend old Jim ever had in the world, and the *only* one he's got now; and then I happened to look around, to see that paper.

It is crucial that Huck remembers not just what Jim has done for him, but what he has done for Jim. Huck's earlier decision and action on Jim's behalf began a momentum in the direction of righteousness that he cannot now undo.[1] Past action shaped and directed future possibilities. Similarly, he is influenced not only by what he thinks of Jim but also by what Jim thinks of him. Bearing the burden of being Jim's best and only friend, Huck must act in light of that relationship. He literally is not free to reason as an objective observer would be. What others in our story think and expect of us is an important factor in what we are and do. Huck, in his reverie, *sees* Jim, and now he "happened to see that paper," and must choose between the two:

> It was a close place. I took it up, and held it in my hand. I was a trembling, because I'd got to decide, forever, betwixt two things, and I knowed it. I studied a minute, sort of holding my breath, and then says to myself:
> "All right, then, I'll *go* to hell"—and tore it up.

Every reader knows Huck has done the right thing and is not going to hell for doing it. The story has told them so, and there is no room for second opinions—neither authoritarian nor relativistic. This is the high point of the novel and of Huck's moral development. That he declines from this height in the long and unsatisfying conclusion to the novel is often noted. Why does Huck, who has learned so much and acted so well, become accomplice to the cruel and dehumanizing games Tom Sawyer plays with Jim at the end?

One answer is that both Twain and Huck lose control of their stories. Tom Sawyer arrives, takes over the story, and Huck dwindles as a character and a moral reasoner. Tom has no meaningful history with Jim, no shared story, and can therefore casually return him to the status of stereotype and slave. Huck's own direct contact with Jim ends, and he no longer has the personal reminder of Jim's humanity and dignity. Both Jim and Huck become thinner and less interesting characters. This is not a cagey strategy on Twain's part to make some subtle moral point, but evidence that writers, like the rest of us, sometimes lose track of the meaning of their stories.

The middle of a story can only be significant if it is connected in meaningful ways to its beginning and end. Frank Kermode claims that "in every plot there is an escape from chronicity" (50). Chronicity is clock time, ticktock, "one damn thing after another" (47). It is succession without progression, or even meaningful cause and effect. It is time dehumanized and devalued, measured by repetition, not by significance.

Even the word we use to describe the sound of a clock, "tick-tock," reveals our hunger for pattern, Kermode argues, our insistence on beginning (tick) and end (tock) (44). The goal of story and of all art—or any meaning system—is to give significance to the interval between tick (beginning) and tock (end), between tick (birth) and tock (death).

The antidote to mere clock time—_chronos_—is _kairos_, the Greek and biblical notion of time redeemed. In classical Greek, kairos referred, among other things, to a decisive time, a moment that required an important decision (Kittel 455). It described the position one was put in by fate that required choice and action. There was a statue to a god named Kairos outside the stadium at Olympia, perhaps in recognition of the need for athletes to seize the moment, to act decisively before the opportunity was past.

Kairos was also linked to the idea of responsibility. One has a duty, in Stoicism for instance, to fulfill the demands of the pregnant moment, and doing so was part of developing one's character. In this sense, as in many others, story time is kairos, not chronos. Characters in story must choose, and are responsible for the consequences of their choices. With choosing comes significance.

The opposite of such choosing and acting in Greek thought was passivity. The Greeks, of course, believed strongly in fate, but that did not mean one waited idly for things to happen. Seizing the moment was an act of faith that one's destiny required and rewarded decisive action. Kairos was an antidote to a fatalism that made one the passive victim of time and chance.

Early Christianity adapted and gave theological richness to the Greek notion of kairos.[2] God is seen as impregnating time with significance throughout salvation history, most notably in the Incarnation. Jesus presents himself in the gospels as the fulfillment of the very purpose of time and history: "The time has come. The kingdom of God is near. Repent and believe the good news!" His life creates a new urgency for everyone who encounters his message: "Now is the

67

acceptable time; now is the day of salvation." This message requires a decision ("Who do you say that I am?") and a changed life ("Why do you call me 'Lord, Lord' and do not do what I say?"), not merely assent or dissent.

Kairos derives its ability to redeem the time, to make time significant rather than merely chronological, by its relation to that which is beyond time—transcendence. Kairos is not transcendence itself, but transcendence intersecting with time and transforming it, creating what T. S. Eliot in *Four Quartets* called "the timeless moment." Eliot felt painfully the emptiness of unredeemed time, as in this description of a ride on the London subway:

> *Here is a place of disaffection*
> *Time before and time after*
> *In a dim light. . . .*
> *Neither plenitude nor vacancy. Only a flicker*
> *Over the strained time-ridden faces*
> *Distracted from distraction by distraction*
> *Filled with fancies and empty of meaning*
> *Tumid apathy with no concentration*
> *Men and bits of paper, whirled by the cold wind*
> *That blows before and after time,*
> *Wind in and out of unwholesome lungs*
> *Time before and time after. . . .*
> *Not here the darkness, in this twittering world.*
> (120)

Eliot believed the only effective remedy for the sad waste time of human futility was the kairos moment when time and transcendence intersect and we are allowed to see into the heart of things. One such timeless moment, among many, may come in prayer.

Transcendence does not have to be divine to give significance to story time, though in many of our shaping stories it is. But it must be something larger and more important than mere materiality and succession. Something has to allow the details of plot to cohere, to hang together, to matter, to form a whole. That something is often the story's ending.

Stories have ends in both senses of the word. End means cessation, the stopping of something, but it also means goal, the target at which something aims. Kermode says that "it is one of the great charms of books [and stories] that they have to end" (23). In a curious way, the beginnings and middles of stories cannot be fully meaningful unless they end. The end is the final working out of all the latent potential of the beginning, and the consequences of choices in the middle. Without that working out, the story risks degenerating into mere succession, "one damn thing after another."

Every choice a character makes is a vote against the chaos of infinite possibilities. In a random world everything is possible but nothing significant is likely. No order exists by which the next thing that occurs is not only somewhat predictable but also more likely to be desirable. Story transforms the useless freedom of chaos into the invaluable freedom of responsibility, and it does so by insisting on the significance of choices.

By truly choosing, a character both limits freedom and gives it value. Each choice limits subsequent possibilities in a way that increases the likelihood for significance, just as pruning a fruit tree limits possibilities for growth but encourages the eventual production of the best fruit. Each choice in the middle reduces the possible endings, but without those choices the end would have no meaning.

It seems curious that something that does not yet exist, the end, can influence that which already exists, the middle. But of course the end does exist before it comes into being. It exists in the latent possibilities of the givens of the beginning and in the working out of those possibilities in the middle. The trajectory of a life—and its end—is created by choices made in the context of the beginning and middle.

That middles affect ends is obvious, but ends can also affect and even shape middles. Most characters, in life and in fiction, have some notion, however hazy or unarticulated, of what would constitute a successful life for them. They have an idea of how they would like to "end up." That idea, that imagined end, can be as powerful as anything in the given of beginnings in determining the direction of our lives.

The power of an imagined end, and it literally can only be imagined, lies in its ability to influence present choices. If as a college freshman I imagine myself a doctor, then I choose to take chemistry and by the choice make that imagined end slightly but perceptibly more possible. If I imagine myself a writer, I begin to write; if a basketball player, I shoot baskets; if a husband and father, I marry; if a friend, I listen; if a believer, I pray. If I can imagine nothing, I do nothing—I choose nothing—and thereby allow my life to degenerate from being a story to being a mere succession of events in a twittering world.

The ends mentioned above are all intermediate ends, ones that can be reached long before life is over. But the influence of the end on the middle is also true of ultimate ends, including those that extend beyond the end of life. One woman, when confronted with an important and risky decision in her life, invokes what she calls her "old woman principle." "When I have to decide whether to do something risky, I ask myself if when I am an old woman in my nineties I will regret having passed up the chance." This woman uses an imagined position at the end of her life to help her live the middle. The same is true for saints, political revolutionaries, social reformers, and nine-to-five pluggers.

Martin Luther King, for instance, gave a speech in a small black church in Montgomery, Alabama, in 1966. He began his speech, as he often did, in low, conversational tones. Casually scratching his head, he said, "I can't stand here tonight without thinking of 1955 and '56." He proceeded then to recount the events of the Montgomery bus boycott that began the greatest wave of the longtime civil rights movement. He then recalled 1960 and the effort to integrate lunch counters in the South, adding, "I'm just referring to a little history now." The people nodded and grunted with growing understanding.

Then he moved to recalling 1961 and the freedom riders who rode buses from Washington, D.C., into the deep South, and who, despite having their bus burned, kept going until segregation had been eliminated from interstate travel. And he added again, "I'm just trying to point out a little history here." By now the audience knew exactly what he was doing and what their role was. He was reenacting sacred history and they were the chorus.

He then moved to 1962 and the mass arrest of black protesters in Albany, Georgia. By now King's voice was no longer low and casual. He was moving into the higher pitch and longer cadences of the black preacher, a voice and a rhythm that spoke in its vibrations alone—never mind its words—of suffering and triumph, of pain and perseverance. And in that soaring voice he chronicled for the faithful the story of Sheriff Bull Connor of Birmingham and his attempts to intimidate those who marched for their freedom:

"He got his dogs, but it wasn't long before he discovered that we had something within that dogs couldn't bite." That's right.

"He got his fire hoses, but it wasn't long after that before he realized we had a fire shut up in our bones that water couldn't put out." Oh yes.

"He got his paddy wagons, but it wasn't long after that before he discovered we had numbers that paddy wagons couldn't hold." Thank you, Jesus.

"He took us to his jails, but it wasn't long after that before . . . he discovered his jails couldn't hold us." The last few words no one heard because the audience had been lifted beyond the need for words, and their prolonged shout proclaimed both a shared past and a shared vision for the future.

King took the succession of years and made them a story by giving them a plot, creating meaning by pointing out significant links between events that might otherwise be seen as merely isolated episodes of pain. And he made it clear that it was not just his story but their story together, a story that had the potential to transform the most pitiful individual story by joining it to the larger story of the community.

71

One reason the civil rights movement has wandered in recent decades is that we have moved from "I have a dream" to "I have a program." Martin Luther King told stories; current leaders cite statistics. Stories engage both the heart and the head and move people to action. Statistics elicit counterstatistics and move people to argue. Stories demand a response (that is, responsibility); statistics encourage a rebuttal.

The key component which guarantees the significance of the various events in King's speech is their common link to an imagined end: a just society. It was an end that had not been realized by 1968 when King was assassinated and is still not realized today. Maybe it never can be fully, but imagining it, and making choices based on it, is one way millions of people the world over have "redeemed the time" and made their lives into a meaningful story.

Our stories are in important ways quest narratives (MacIntyre 219). In classic quest narratives the hero journeys through great perils to accomplish the quest—Jason to capture the Golden Fleece, the Knights of the Round Table to find the Holy Grail, Ahab to get his revenge on the white whale. Many of the perils are external—dragons, whirlpools, giants—but the most terrible and difficult are internal—fear, indulgence, and self-delusion.

Quests require a goal, something for which to quest. Identifying such goals, even in general terms, increases one's odds of living a meaningful story. King accomplished so much, in part, because he had so clear an understanding of the end toward which he was working and living.

But the ends toward which our stories tend are not always so clear. Often, as we saw earlier, the hero discovers in the process of the quest that the seeming goal is not the real goal. As MacIntyre points out, the true goal of the quest is frequently realized only during the process of questing, not before. We choose to act, and in the acting discover its ultimate meaning—eventually, maybe. Living in this way is an act of faith, faith that the universe is so constructed that meaningful stories are realistic possibilities, not cowardly escapism.

Because a fuller understanding of the ultimate meaning of our story comes only through living it, it is important that we not postpone significant action in the middle for lack of complete knowledge about our ends. Incomplete knowledge and lack of certainty are not valid excuses for inaction. Huck chose to help Jim earn his freedom despite powerful doubts that he was doing the right thing and about the fate of his own soul. Martin Luther King had no idea when he began the bus boycott in Montgomery in 1956 that it would be anything more than a local response to a local grievance. By acting in small things with very partial knowledge, characters enlarge their stories and discover both who they are and what their lives can mean.

Our actions help us discover our ends, and our imagined ends help shape our actions. If we have no sense of our lives having a plot, being a meaningful story, we are unlikely to imagine a significant goal for them, and therefore less likely to act purposefully in the long middle. One of the happy outcomes of the various human rights movements of the twentieth century has been the expanded possibilities for millions of people to imagine better stories and endings for themselves.

But can we really work up all this faith in story at this point in human history? Might not all this be mere wishful thinking or circular reasoning? There is widespread skepticism, especially among intellectuals, about any and all attempts to posit a fundamental order or meaning for human experience. Such attempts are seen as naive, or sentimental, or even authoritarian. Speaking about life as a story may express our *desire* for meaning, but it is only whistling in the dark.

Even some storytellers have lately abandoned traditional notions of story. The so-called postmodernists in particular create fictions that emphasize dislocation, disjunction, and absurdity. They reject the idea of beginning, middle, and end—Aristotle be hanged. Their stories begin by mocking the idea of stories beginning, calling attention to themselves as made-up—and therefore trivial—things. Their

73

middles reject meaningful connections between events. Cause divorces effect, reducing actions to arbitrary or endless, repetitive exercises in futility. Stories don't end, especially not in any way that would imply a shape to things; they simply stop, the more ambiguously the better. Or better yet, they trail off, limping into the void. John Barth's "Lost in the Funhouse" self-consciously comments on its own (intentional) failure to cohere as a story: "the plot doesn't rise by meaningful steps but winds upon itself, digresses, retreats, hesitates, sighs, collapses, expires" (96).

Are these stories, too? Of course they are. And we should value them. They are a healthy reminder that we cannot take order and meaning for granted. They testify, as art has always done, to the dark shadow that can fall at any time across any life, not just the shadow of misfortune, but of the sense that things don't fit, that, as Camus argued, the longings of our hearts are not compatible with the way life is (16). For if story was not big enough to include disorder as well as order, absurdity as well as meaning, skepticism as well as belief, then it would not be big enough.

If your story is one of disconnectedness, then that is the story you must tell. But do not be surprised if in the telling that sense of disconnectedness is eased. Because if you tell that story sincerely, we will listen, and maybe tell you our own story in return. And then, if we all allow it, we will at least feel connected to each other, for we will have shared our stories.

The traditional literary form best suited to contain the perception that "the time is out of joint" is tragedy. Tragedy ends in death, defeat, and disappointed dreams. It considers, with Hamlet, the possibility that this life is "an unweeded garden / That grows to seed," filled with "things rank and gross" (1.2.135–36). And that

this goodly frame, the earth, seems to me a sterile promontory; this most excellent canopy, the air, look you, this brave o'erhanging firmament, this majestical roof fretted with golden fire, why, it appears no other thing to me than a foul and pestilent congregation of vapours. What a piece of work is a man!

how noble in reason! how infinite in faculty! in form and moving
how express and admirable! in action how like an angel! in
apprehension how like a god! the beauty of the world! the para-
gon of animals! and yet, to me, what is this quintessence of
dust? man delights not me . . . (2.2.292–302)

Why then do we so often feel uplifted at the end of a performance of tragedy. One suggestion is that we can face the
brokenness and seeming pessimism of tragedy exactly because it has
been embodied in a dramatic narrative. We take comfort that even
the worst life has to offer can be given a shape, can be expressed—
enacted—and therefore contemplated and reconciled.

Even our contemporary fiction of disjointedness and disjuncture
depends for its effect on being the exception. These stories interest
us, if only mildly, because they perform their tricks against a pan-
orama of traditional stories that are more willing to take leaps of
faith. If these more cynical stories were the *only* ones available to us
we would be quickly bored and turn to dominoes to pass the time.
That they successfully disappoint our desire for connectedness and
meaning only testifies to how fundamental that desire is. Art won't
get far by ignoring or ridiculing that or any other human desire.

Reynolds Price contrasts a traditional Judeo-Christian understanding of the human story that insists on God's benevolent
relationship to his creation despite his hiddenness with a popular
contemporary alternative: "I am here alone, there is no one beyond
me, I will soon dissolve" (23–24). The latter stories, when they are
stories at all, are literally intolerable, Price argues, not only because
we want the world to be otherwise but because except in our
bleakest moments they strike us as false (25). Such a view of life has
been contemplated throughout human history—Ecclesiastes offers
one example—but has always been found both false and unlivable.
If we have lost the confidence to call anything false, it is still true
that one cannot honestly base a life on such a view.

One cannot conclusively prove rationally that the perception of a
meaningful plot to one's life is not simply wishing. The only relevant

proof is the quality of life lived. If I believe there is a plot to my life, and I act in accordance with that belief, then in fact I can achieve a kind of order and significance whether I should be able to or not. Those who deny this, and who believe life is random and ultimately meaningless, had better live lives that are consistent with that belief and are superior to my own. And if they desperately resort to the old definition game ("What do you mean by superior?"), then we can justly conclude they have nothing to offer us of practical value.

While insisting on the legitimacy of meaningful imagined ends, we must also admit their limits and possible misuse. Imagined ends, while powerful, are always provisional—and should be. Sometimes the experiences of life reveal those goals to be inadequate, even warped. In Eliot's version of Thomas à Becket's life, the saint has to fight against manipulating a martyred end for himself that would violate his own faith. The tempter who counsels him to seek a glorious death asks,

> *What can compare with glory of Saints*
> *Dwelling forever in presence of God? . . .*
> *Seek the way of martyrdom, make yourself the lowest*
> *On earth, to be high in heaven. (Murder 192)*

Becket recognizes this proposed end for what it is and, not without difficulty, resists the impure motive even as he accepts the fate: "The last temptation is the greatest treason: / To do the right thing for the wrong reason" (196).

We can modify our stories while we are living them because we are both characters and co-creators. There is an ongoing tension between living as our stories dictate as opposed to dictating the stories we live. We both shape and are shaped by stories.

In fact, we help create even the stories we read or hear from others. Henry James argued that the novelist uses relatively few details to give the *impression* of offering an entire world. The reader is the one who fills in all that is missing or only implied. The reader hears the tone of voice, guesses at motivations not explicitly stated, creates faces for characters not described, and makes connections and draws conclusions the author may or may not have intended.

This self-making quality of story is important because ultimately we listen to, embrace, and help create the stories we feel we need. For the truth, as we saw earlier, "is not simply what happened but how we felt about it when it was happening, and how we feel about it now" (Rouse 99). For all the rationalist's distrust of subjectivity, we cannot escape the fact that anything we know we know as limited subjects, as individuals trying to strike a livable balance between the demands of the outer and inner worlds. Though born into stories not of our own choosing, we have thereafter an ever expanding ability to select among those stories, to choose new ones, and to alter our stories by the way we participate in their working out.

Reynolds Price explains in retrospect his decision to set aside other work and translate certain biblical narratives into English: "In a hard time I was turning to the inscribed bases of beliefs which had supported me and my family. The stories I was choosing were the stories I needed. . . . The root of story sprang from need—need for companionship and consolation by a creature as vulnerable, four million years ago and now, as any protozoan in a warm brown swamp. The need is not for the total consolation of narcotic fantasy . . . but for credible news that our lives proceed in order toward a pattern which, if tragic here and now, is ultimately pleasing . . ." (13–14).

What is "ultimately pleasing" for Price is the reality of a just God who knows us. But those who do not believe in such a God still seek something bigger than themselves around which to build their story. Belief in nothing is barely compatible with life, and impossible if one's life is going to seem valuable: "Wholehearted commitment in life and in myth requires a fundamental _faith_ in some aspect of the human enterprise. Condemned to be free, adults must transcend their angst to find something in life to believe in. The stories we live by are enhanced by our faith and our fidelity to something larger and nobler than the self—be that something God, the human spirit, progress through technology, or some other transcendent end" (Mc-Adams 174).

We are most likely to find something like this within story. With its belief in choice; in purposeful human actions; in connections between the past, present, and future; and in its commitment to meaningful (not necessarily happy) endings, story is our best testimony to the faith that we are more than the sum of the atoms that form us, and that, all things considered, life is preferable to death.

5

Seeing the World Through Stories: Stories and the Shaping of a Worldview

We tell stories because we desire a world with a story.
Michael Edwards

Religions commit suicide when they find their inspiration in dogmas.
The inspiration of religion lies in . . . history.
Alfred North Whitehead

. . . . it is impossible to tell an audience a story it does not wish to hear.
Reynolds Price

Each of us has a personal canon of sacred stories. These stories helped form what we believe to be true about the world now, and will largely determine what we will come to believe is true in the future. We cannot fundamentally change ourselves without changing our stories. When young, as this canon is being created, we will fairly readily exchange some core stories for others. As we get older, we tend to defend our sacred stories the way Davy Crockett defended the Alamo, preferring to die with our stories rather than surrender them for alien ones.

The most intractable conflicts in both our personal and public lives result from the collisions of contrary and incompatible stories. Pro-life versus pro-choice, Northern Irish Catholic versus Protestant, Palestinian versus Israeli, socialist versus capitalist, environmentalist versus developer, daughter and son versus mother and father, estranged wife versus husband—in all these cases and many more, stories are the animating force for strongly held values and beliefs, and stories are the primary factor in their successful or unsuccessful resolution.

Facts and reason alone do not stand a chance against a story because both depend on story for their power. It is naive to think one has arrived at one's views and values solely through unbiased consideration of objective data. Data are never objective because they are always gathered by story-breathing human subjects. All facts are inert and useless until they have been interpreted, integrated into this narrative or that.

Furthermore, the same facts may serve opposing stories equally well. The rate of poverty in America, one argues, proves that the oppressive free-market system is not working and must be drastically modified by government intervention. The rate of poverty in America, another argues, proves that the genius of free-market economics is hindered by big government interference which must be eliminated. Argue either case solely with statistics and charts and we will nod politely as we nod off to sleep. Augment that case with powerful stories of hungry children or freeloading welfare cheats and we will storm the barricades.

The inevitably subjective quality of facts and reason does not prove that truth is relative, only that our understanding of it is conditioned by story. Story provides reason a context within which to work, and without that context reason is an amoral mercenary, ready to serve any ideology. Detached from humanizing story, reason is as content to fill gas chambers as to fill the stomachs of the hungry. Stories, of course, also can be distorted and misused—all the more reason to encourage healthy stories.

Most forms of persuasion depend on narrative. Politics, for instance, is the art of selling stories. In the United States, political parties and ideologies basically tell us their story of America, each with its distinctive themes, characters, plot, symbols, and tone. One story is America as the land of opportunity, the home of the free and the brave, the place where success is determined by innate talents and hard work. Another story counters that America is a place founded on oppression and exploitation, first of the Native Americans and then of Africans, followed by the immigrant poor of Europe and Asia, and at all times of women. In other stories we portray ourselves to ourselves as lovers of freedom, independence, the underdog; as defenders of the weak and oppressed; as champions of democracy. Likewise, we lacerate ourselves with stories of our love of violence, and of our penchant for domination and exploitation.

The characters in these shared public stories are many and varied, some historical, some imagined. They include Pilgrims and Indians (each alternately glorified or vilified at different times in history), Lincoln and Lee, Uncle Tom and Sojourner Truth, robber barons and muckrakers, war heroes and traitors, Mickey Mantle and Marilyn Monroe.

Like all stories, these public stories and characters change with time, and with changing values and prejudices. It was clear to me as a first-grader in the 1950s that the Pilgrims were good guys, to be admired for their faith in God, their perseverance, and for inviting the Indians to dinner. That version of the story can no longer be told in school—almost literally when it comes to their religious faith. The story may no longer illustrate God's providence, but only how people get along better when they cooperate (you might call it the _Sesame Street_ version of American history). If anything, the Pilgrims are now morally suspect, first for initiating the theft of the continent from the Indians, and second for intolerantly believing their God and their values were better than other gods and values.

_81_

The same facts with different tellers yield different stories. At the heart of the contemporary culture wars in America is the battle over who will tell which stories and how. Every group will borrow and shape these public stories to tell their version of America at any one time. And the one who does it most persuasively will win the battle for hearts and minds—and elections.

"But what about the facts? What about the data I've collected? They show clearly that . . ." It is not mere cynicism to claim that the facts often show exactly what the user of facts wants them to show, and what the target of the facts is willing to let them show. I don't wish to exaggerate this. We can at times be persuaded to change our views and actions based on the reasoned presentation of evidence. Facts and reason can be a check against pure illusion, but they are not the trump cards some assume. We are rightly suspicious of all so-called facts (those hard nuggets of uncontested data) until we know how they are going to be used, and we can only begin to know that when we know the story into which they are being integrated.

If I believe abortion to be the killing of the most helpless of all human beings, I am very unlikely to be moved by mountains of facts about the welfare costs of unwanted children, lost wages for working mothers, or closely reasoned arguments about hidden rights in the Constitution. If I believe abortion an exercise of one of the most fundamental human rights—that of sovereignty over one's own body —and a long-overdue correction of the abuse of women, then what do I care about intricate arguments about when life begins, or fetal brain development, or tenuous historical analogies to slavery and Hitler?

A person taking any position on this intractable moral and social problem likely had his or her initial thinking shaped by story, and certainly has had that position reinforced by story thereafter. My own position first began taking shape in a speech class in college in the middle 1960s, at a time before abortion was legal and when, for a naive freshman male, the issue was totally abstract. I was equally happy to debate whichever side of the issue I was assigned, and glibly (and successfully) offered arguments and repeated slogans I now believe totally spurious.

That initial glibness, marshaled impressively with facts, began to wane when a friend had her first abortion, and then a second—and later a third. It eroded further when my wife helped out an unmarried Native American girl who was pregnant without a husband or supporting family. Subsequent contact with an organization working at the heart of this issue exposed me to the stories of many women, and some men, whose life experience did not make the issue simple for me, but did make very clear on which side I must work.

At no point in this process did I abandon reason or facts. I thought as clearly and logically as I could. But others, also claiming logic, have come to opposite conclusions. Why? In part because of the inevitable imprecision and subjectivity of reason, but also because of the different stories they have embraced, and the specific interpretation they have given to their own experience. Any view we have of the world gives us an appetite for further stories that confirm that view of the world and a distaste for those which do not.

A story is indestructible unless the one who embraces the story chooses to destroy it. It cannot be successfully falsified solely by outside enemies. This is true in the reputedly objective world of science as well as in the overwhelmingly subjective world of interpersonal relations. Scientists and feuding couples alike reveal their humanity in selectively choosing and shaping their facts, often unconsciously, to fit a preexisting story of how things are. In my family there is a story about which everyone agrees that a piece of crockery was thrown, but the two combatants have exactly opposite memories of who threw it at whom. Each needs to remember it a certain way in order to sustain her story of her place in the family.

Stories (and facts) are so malleable because we do not simply remember them, we help create them. Elizabeth Stone observes, "The facts of a family's past can be selectively fashioned into a story that can mean almost anything, whatever they most need it to mean" (17). From the infinite stream of data and impressions that flow through us we choose here and there, a little of this and a little of that, to weave together the stories we need to form a coherent picture of the world and our place in it.

Dan McAdams suggests that everyone develops a personal myth of self-explanation—and he calls this process an act of the imagination (12). Calling it an act of the imagination does not mean, as some might surmise, that such a personal myth is wholly "made up" or false, or the opposite of fact or reason. The created myth or story is simply the best way of holding all the facts together in a way that makes sense and allows one to operate in the world.

Identifying the core stories by which we define our values and our views can serve, in fact, as a reality check and as a measure of our integrity. If our experience repeatedly clashes with our defining stories, we may be led to change our stories. Similarly, if we too often or too drastically diverge in our daily actions from the story we claim, our allegiance to the story should (and often does) prompt us to modify our actions.

An old-fashioned term for this prompting is guilt. If we behaved in a way that violated the values of our defining stories, we felt guilty about it and that guilt was a prompt to correct our actions. Modern psychology has banned a positive conception of guilt, but such a mechanism, whatever we call it, is found in every human culture and is critical to any moral order. Without it no human rights movement could ever succeed. Martin Luther King pointed out to America the great discrepancy between the song it sang about itself —"the land of the free and the home of the brave"—and the reality for African-Americans. He kept pointing it out until America was forced either to change its behavior or to change its story.

The main check on fraudulent or distorted stories is not isolated facts, but other stories. You cannot generally argue individuals or societies out of their story, destructive though it may be, unless there is a better one with which to replace it. We need to visualize things differently before we are willing to act differently. "The devil you know is better than the devil you don't know" expresses our preference for familiar pain over uncertainty. Broken stories can be replaced with healthier ones if the latter are powerful enough to overcome our innate reluctance to change our stories.

In sum, the common distinction between mere stories and "the real world" is naive. Stories _compose_ the real world. We cannot form a picture of our experience without them. Stories not only are based on experience, they _become_ part of the experience of the reader or hearer. A story is something that _happens to you,_ as much as a car wreck or job promotion. I didn't just read _Huckleberry Finn_ at various times in my life, I experienced it. Like Robert Coles's young patient, I was on the raft with Huck and Jim, using the same powers of the mind and imagination that I use in listening to a political speech, or a sermon, or my daughter's questions about life. Because I experienced that story, I am a slightly different person. That story affected my mind and spirit, that which is essentially me, and therefore had more impact than any merely physical event from "the real world."

The stories that create our views and values must meet certain minimum requirements. The first is that they explain. They must explain our experience, external and internal. The least livable life is the one without coherence—nothing connects, nothing means anything. Stories make connections. They allow us to see our past, our present, and our future as interrelated and purposeful. We seek out stories which enhance this process.

It is not enough that our stories explain our experience; that explanation must also be satisfying. We embrace those stories which create a world in which we find it possible, even desirable, to live. The stories need not be happy, but they must be meaningful. The stories we value most reassure us that life is worth the pain, that meaning is not an illusion, and that others share our experience with us. Consider the frequent claim among World War II veterans that their years in the service were "the best years of my life." Never before or after did most live with such hardship, lack of physical comforts, psychological stress, violence, and danger of sudden death. Yet they felt themselves part of a large and important story, one that gave meaning to their own. Contrast that common feeling with that of many Vietnam veterans, equally courageous but participants in a war with no coherent plot or satisfying ending.

If our stories must be satisfying, the most satisfying stories are the ones we not only tell but in which we participate. Our most important stories affect how we behave. One workable definition of a hypocrite is a person who does not actively live out the stories he or she claims to value. Michael Root argues that "significance is a function of the relation between the story and the world or life of the reader" (147). A story is insignificant to us when it plays no role in how we live. A profoundly significant one reorders our life.

Is a particular story important? Only to the extent that you choose to participate in it. Even the most powerful and affirming story becomes significant to me only when it moves from being *a* story to being *my* story. That is why the acid test for any movement —religious, political, social—is whether or not the next generation of adherents will embrace and give continued life to the stories of the founders.

One particular life which illustrates many of the things we have been saying is that of Augustine. Over 1,500 years ago Augustine wrote what may be the first autobiography in the modern sense. Rather than offering a rational explanation of his conversion to Christianity, as might be expected of a man of his education and training, he chose to tell the story of his life. In his *Confessions,* Augustine depicts himself trying out different life stories with their attendant values and behaviors. He is at various times the young, indulgent rake; the philosophical intellectual; and the ambitious careerist. But despite his undeniable successes, he was desperately unhappy. "I was led astray myself and led others astray in my turn. We were alike deceivers and deceived in all our different aims and ambitions, both publicly when we expounded our so-called liberal ideas, and in private through our service to what we called religion. In public we were cocksure, in private superstitious, and everywhere void and empty" (71; bk.4.1).

Augustine eventually became a Christian not primarily through the power of rational argument, but because he decided (with both his mind and his emotions) that Christianity was a better story. His mother, Monica, had been pressing the Christian story on him since his childhood, but there are some stories a young man will not hear from his mother. He had likewise heard the story from undereducated Christian apologists who tried to defeat him intellectually, but he had delighted in tying them up in rhetorical knots. A turning point for Augustine was hearing the story from a man whom he respected intellectually and who treated Augustine as a human being, not as an enemy to be defeated. Augustine recalled his initial experience with Ambrose, bishop of Milan: "This man of God received me like a father and, as bishop, told me how glad he was that I had come. My heart warmed to him, not at first as a teacher of the truth, which I had quite despaired of finding in your Church, but simply as a man who showed me kindness. I listened attentively when he preached to the people" (107; bk.5.13).

Augustine eventually traded the shaping stories of his youth for the story of Christian faith. That act changed not only what he believed but how he conceived of himself, how he related to the world and to God, and what he should do in life. He literally changed who he was, becoming a different character in a different story. His personality may have remained largely the same, but his more essential character was forever different.

Augustine gave authority to a new story and made it his story. In so doing he accepted as authoritative a whole canon of attendant stories—from the Bible and from church history and from the lives of fellow believers, including his mother. He reread his own life in light of those stories. Because his defining story was now different, the stories of his own life changed, including those of his past. T. S. Eliot claims that a genuinely groundbreaking work in literature today changes works of the past because the new work causes us to see past works differently (5). The same occurs when we accept a new defining story for our life. Nothing—past, present, or future—looks the same.

We readily accept that religious people embrace a set of stories as authoritative. In fact, some fault them for doing so too uncritically. But everyone, religious and nonreligious alike, has sacred stories. Hauerwas and Burrell "wonder whether everyone does not accept a set of stories as canonical. To identify those stories would be to discover the shape one's basic convictions take" (39). Our essential orientation to life is a consequence of the stories that form us. Our values and convictions are expressed best in stories because stories preserve the memory of characters making choices.

When I look at the many stories that have shaped my own life, I am struck by how many different stories I have lived simultaneously. Although we may have one essential character, we have a variety of personas—performances of that character—that vary from context to context. As a teenager I participated in a number of different worlds. I was the good, churchgoing kid; the bright student; but also the quasi-athlete, hanging out with the boys. I moved among these different roles—note the story origin of the word "roles"—with unconscious ease. When I went from the physics lab at the end of the school day to the gym for basketball practice, my vocabulary and intonations unconsciously changed. The stories of the classroom gave way to the lore and dialect of the court ("You shoulda seen the way he deeked him with a head fake and then jammed in that sucker's face"). I even walked and held my body differently. To the present day my wife claims she can tell when an old friend has called me long-distance by the way my voice and cadence on the phone change to match the ones we shared many years ago.

My point is not just the obvious one that we all play many different roles, but that each of these roles is story-formed. I knew what was expected of me as a churchgoing kid because of dozens of stories that defined that role for me. My church stories, for instance, were big on sacrifice. I got the distinct impression that being a good Christian was likely to get me killed, or at least severely ridiculed (worse than death for an adolescent). Isaac got off at the last second when his dad was about to do him in, but how about Paul, and Stephen, and *all* the disciples except one? Not to mention Christ himself. This was a bloody business. And in case I thought maybe all this was in the distant past, there were bushels of current stories of dugout canoes, Auca Indians, and martyred missionaries. No question about it, I should expect trouble in the world. (And *not* being persecuted was a bad sign, too.)

Likewise, I wouldn't have known how to be a Dodger fan without Dodger stories. Though I didn't start following them until the late 1950s, I needed to know of their heartbreaking losses to the Yankees in the early 1950s. I needed to know how wild Sandy Koufax had been in his early years before becoming a master of control. (And if you don't know whether I'm talking about his lifestyle or his curveball, then you don't share these stories.) I collected and relished the stories not only of the stars—Koufax, Snider, Wills—but also of the minor characters—Pignatano, Moon, and Repulski. And because I possess this storehouse of stories, I have instant rapport with anyone who followed my team from the mid-1950s to the mid-1970s.

Though the importance of story in religion and sports may appear special cases, it is equally fundamental to every significant area of life: parenting, being a husband or wife, politics, profession, intellectual and aesthetic pursuit, and so on. Our marriages are surrounded by the stories of the marriages in which we were raised, our professions are the accumulated stories of past professionals in our field, our ideas are in constant dialogue with the narrated ideas of the past and present. We inherit and participate in these stories, adding our own to the collection.

Because our stories are so varied and so powerful, we must forge some kind of workable relationship among these story clusters if we are to be healthy and whole. In my own case this has required integrating two story streams that often flowed together in the past but which are widely seen as incompatible today. If pressed for a label, I would call myself a religious humanist, more specifically a Christian humanist. It was only as an adult that I consciously understood what I felt in my bones even as a child—faith and learning could go together, but beware of letting these respective storytellers know about the other.

I grew up, you see, among the fundamentalists. Fundamentalists are more varied than the media stereotype would suggest, but in my formative years I lived among the type that give liberals night sweats. These were the kind of people who often thought of college as the place one lost one's faith in Jesus. If they didn't understand or want to understand the world of books and ideas, that other world returned the favor. I was eventually to feel like a man with his legs in two different and diverging rowboats, not able to pull his foot out of either without ending up in deep water.

When I reflect on the stories that contributed to whatever I am today, I immediately realize they are too many to enumerate—even to myself. Still, it might be possible to isolate a few to illustrate the process. One of my defining qualities, I now see, is a penchant for viewing the world through moral criteria. I have an instinctive fondness for the categories of good and evil, right and wrong, that verges at times on the moralistic. I never consciously decided to see the world this way (though I have consciously decided as an adult not to abandon it). I believe I developed this habit of perception because a steady stream of stories, secular and sacred, presented reality to me in these terms.

A powerful common theme in stories from my childhood and after centered on good and evil, punishment and reward, and the consequences of choices—especially the bad consequences of bad choices, which were much easier to visualize and seemed more certain to a child than happy ones. An early source was fairy tales, sometimes as filtered through Disney. Fairy tales offered a simplified and yet accurate view of the world where it mattered who you ran around with and what you did. Because Pinocchio listened to the wrong people he ended up with donkey ears, and was saved only through conscience and courage. Because two of the three pigs preferred to play before they worked, they ended up as lunch meat for the Big Bad Wolf.

I moved easily between Pinocchio in the belly of Monstro and Jonah in the belly of the whale. Some from my fundamentalist past would lament the confusion between what they take as mere imagination versus hard-core, historical reality. I see both as embodying similar truths and therefore as allies. Pinocchio didn't obey and paid the price. Jonah was assigned a bad territory to work—Nineveh—and he chose to ignore the assignment. Bad choice. God, it appears, gives commands, not suggestions (one reason among many why he is out of fashion).

It was clear to me as a child that donkey ears and whale bellies were just around the corner depending on my choices. I still see the dim light in the empty hallway of my second-grade Texas school. I had been sent to run an errand and as I passed the principal's office I glanced cautiously in the open door, as one might when passing the cave mouth of a local troll. There, through a second open door, I saw a boy bent over holding his ankles and the principal swinging a long, broad paddle. The sound of that paddle was the voice of God to me, saying, "You, Danny Taylor, living in the Baptist preacher's parsonage—I know you and I know what you think about. There's a paddle waiting here with your name on it." Actually, it wasn't so much the voice of God as the combined voice of my Sunday-school teacher, the school principal, and various other adults in my life. But I wasn't worrying about fine distinctions.

If the story of Jonah was reinforced by Disney and school paddlings, it also found its echo in terrifying little Christmas songs. I took very seriously the one that goes: "You better watch out / You better not cry / You better not shout / I'm telling you why. / Santa Claus is coming to town." That was bad enough. But what was far worse? He _knows!_ "He knows when you've been sleeping / He knows when you're awake / He knows when you've been bad or good / so be good for goodness' sake!" There it was, our greatest desire and worst fear: to be known. Somebody was watching—good news. Somebody was watching—bad news. Good news or bad, it mattered what you did, maybe even what you thought. Both had consequences.

One particularly onerous consequence was the effect of my behavior on the Dodgers. I was convinced as a ten-year-old that there was a direct connection between my moral life and the place of the Dodgers in the standings. Cheat on a spelling test and Duke Snider will strike out with the bases loaded. Memorize the Bible verse for Sunday school and he lines it into right field for the winning hit.

The inescapable consequences of choices was a steady drumbeat at home, at church, at school, and on the ball field. You do this, you get that. What goes up must come down. For every action, there is an equal and opposite reaction. You reap what you sow. Ding is followed by dong. My life was one unending lesson in cause and effect.

Some of these lessons were silly in their application ("Do you want to be caught in a movie theater when Jesus comes back?"), but not in their underlying principle (it matters what you fill your mind with). Their aim was to make me a better person. It is not too much to say that their aim was to instruct me in being human. Animals live by instinct and by satisfying basic needs; humans add making choices and accepting responsibility.

As I got older, the stories continued unabated. In sixth grade they were colored baby blue. I remember clearly a seemingly endless series of bite-sized biographies of famous Americans, all bound in baby-blue covers. I read them for extra credit (credit, credit) in sixth grade. Nathan Hale (points) regretted having only one life to give for his country; John Paul Jones (points) defiantly declared to his more powerful enemies, "Don't tread on me"; Abraham Lincoln (more points) was so determined to learn despite his poverty that he did arithmetic on the back of a shovel with pieces of coal. I read for the points, but I was formed by the stories. And all those stories were essentially one story: work hard, have courage, sacrifice for others, do good. In sum, live by and for high values. Hopelessly oversimplified, touchingly naive—absolutely essential. The lack of such naiveté today is killing us.

The stories at church deepened over the years. "Jesus loves me, this I know, for the Bible tells me so" was joined by the Jesus who commanded leaving mother and father to follow him. (Could _that_ be necessary? good?) The ubiquitous stories of missionaries (which have largely disappeared in some denominations because of embarrassment over cultural imperialism) took an uncomfortably personal bent. I was almost sure I was going to have to be one.

My reasoning went something like this: I could either do what I wanted to do with my life (grow up to play for the Dodgers) or do what God wanted me to do with my life (something that required wearing a suit). One of the things I least wanted to do was be a missionary. That, therefore, was the thing God obviously would require of me to stay out of hell.

The place I associated most clearly with missionaries was Africa. My image of Africa was formed less by missionary slides (a dozen or so black people standing stiffly in front of a mission station with two or three white people) than by stories from popular culture: Tarzan, Jungle Jim, Sheena—Queen of the Jungle. If God makes me be a missionary, I thought, I will end up in Africa. And if I end up in Africa, I will eventually end up flat on my back with a spear point at my throat. And this huge, frightening African holding the spear will ask me a question: "Do you believe in Jesus?"

This was a scenario, a story, I played out in my head many times. This imagined fateful moment, spear at my throat, was Nathan Hale, Horatio at the bridge, and the apostle Stephen all rolled into one. (If I hadn't been Baptist, I might have thought of Joan of Arc or some other saint as well.) At that moment I would be forced to make a choice that would determine my ultimate fate. I would say, "Yes, I believe in Jesus," and would be immediately thrust through the throat, ascending then to heaven on the wings of angels shouting, "Glory to St. Dan in the highest." Or—and what a deadly _or_—I would say, "Jesus? No. Don't believe I've heard of any Jesus." And then, of course, I would be spared—for the moment. I would live, but I would live knowing I had failed the test—the big choice—and my life would be haunted and my afterlife too grim to contemplate.

As with worrying about Jesus finding you at the movies, this story I created from a patchwork of received stories was childish in its details, but not in its underlying conception of life. It does matter what I or anyone decides about ultimate things, including God. It does matter whether we live by our values when doing so does not seem in our immediate best interest. At such crucial points—in bedrooms, boardrooms, classrooms, and concentration camps— more than one person has been guided by a story, a story that told them that what they decided mattered.

One of the most widely told stories from the Nazi death camps is of the self-sacrifice of Father Maximilian Kolbe. Imprisoned in Auschwitz for his resistance to the Nazis, Father Kolbe and the rest of his block were lined up in front of their barracks one day in 1941. One of their members had managed to escape, and as punishment every tenth man was to be executed. The count went through the ranks and the man next to Father Kolbe was chosen. In fear and anguish the man cried, "What will happen to my wife, my children?" Father Kolbe spoke out, requesting that he be allowed to take the man's place. The officer in charge agreed, and Kolbe was placed with others in a starvation cell. After days of great suffering, he was murdered with a lethal injection.

Father Kolbe could do what he did only by seeing himself as part of an all-important story in which he was a character with responsibilities. Some have denied that Father Kolbe is worthy of praise because of his own anti-Semitism before the war. These are sins which must not be passed over and for which he must account. But the least that can be said for him is that in this one moment in Auschwitz, if in no other, he lived up to the story of Christ by which every Christian should define his or her life.

The stories I heard at church came not only from the Bible and the pulpit but also on Wednesday nights from the old-timers. In the Bible Belt serious Christians wanted more of God than they could get on Sundays. They gathered, in small but significant numbers, on Wednesday nights for prayer meetings. Even a small sanctuary seemed mostly empty on these nights, the voices echoing in a way they never did on Sunday morning.

Living among people who believe talking to God changes the world's details created in me a strange mix of hopefulness and skepticism. Could it be that God really cared about my book report or my sick friend? If he could make sick people well, why did I have to ask him—wasn't he paying attention? But if these two or three dozen grown-ups (sometimes fewer if the weather was bad) thought it was the right thing to do, there must be something to it.

Their prayers were often in narrative form, but they did more than pray. They told stories. Because Wednesday nights were also testimony time. At some point in the service, people were invited to share spontaneously what God had done in their lives in the last week or so. No one had to prepare for this in advance. There were no notes or three-point outlines. The Spirit was supposed to direct. In fact, the Spirit was ultimately the storyteller.

So after a few moments of silence, and maybe a little prodding from the pastor ("God's not doing much these days, huh?"), someone would inevitably begin. "Well, I just want to thank the Lord for an answer to prayer . . ." And then the storytelling would commence. They would tell stories of suffering relieved, needs met, comfort offered, direction provided, and failures forgiven. Sometimes they asked forgiveness themselves from someone else in the room; sometimes they wept. And everyone in the room helped them tell the story. A quiet "yes" from the person in the pew behind, an "amen" from the corner, a smile and a nod from across the room.

As I write these words I am surprised to feel a rising wave of emotion. Why? Is it simple nostalgia for lost childhood? Not entirely. There is something appropriately moving about a group of simple people coming together to get help for their often difficult existence through sharing the common story of their faith as it works itself out in the individual stories of their lives. I can remember even now the sense of awe and gratefulness I would feel as I, a child, watched from a dark corner while the adults in my life made themselves vulnerable before God and each other. An old carpenter, a young schoolteacher, a white-haired grandmother, the father of my best friend. Before this they lived in a world outside my own, above and beyond me in every meaningful way. In thirty minutes they would be in that world again. But in the brief moment of their story sharing they would become real and human and knowable. He was no longer the Sunday-school superintendent whom you dodged when cutting class. He was the man weeping because his brother had survived the surgery following the car accident. She was not the woman who sold you doughnuts at the bakery. She was the one thanking God for the $25 Christmas bonus so she could pay the rent. Separate individuals—more or less dull, with the usual short-comings and pettinesses—transformed for a moment by the power of shared stories.

As I moved out of childhood and through adolescence into the late teenage years, my storehouse of stories grew. As before, many of them concerned good and evil, right and wrong. I watched the civil rights movement unfold on television, and wondered how this could be happening in my country and what I was supposed to do about it and why no one was saying anything about it at my church. I saw people being knocked off their feet with fire hoses and bitten by vicious dogs, but I couldn't make sense out of it until I heard how all this fit in with a bigger story. What I understand now is that the bigger story made possible the movement. People literally could not have put themselves in front of those hoses and those dogs without the animating power of their collective story. And those who led them drew their authority, in no small part, from their ability to tell that story truly and well.

The stories unfolding in front of me—the civil rights movement, Vietnam, the race to the moon—were matched by stories develop-ing within me. For the first time I became conscious not just of stories but of writers—Twain, Hawthorne, Irving, Dickens in the early years; Camus, Melville, Thoreau, Faulkner, Tolstoy later on. They and their stories became grist for my mental grindings. They presented me not only new worlds but new ways to see my existing world.

And these new ways of seeing the world were often not congenial to my old ways. I wasn't sure whether Twain was contemptuous of the idea of God or only of the people who claimed to worship him, but I knew for sure that _The Mysterious Stranger_ explained the problem of evil in a way my Sunday-school teachers would not have approved. (And what motivated my fourth-grade teacher to read us that story, anyway?)

Similarly, Camus, years later, not only made it clear he didn't believe in God, he left me feeling I was cheating somehow if I did. He seemed clinically honest. He, too, talked about choices and integrity and defining yourself by what you actually did in the world. My Sunday-school teachers not only would have disapproved of him, they wouldn't have understood what he was saying. And sometimes I wished I didn't understand either.

Fortunately, not too long after discovering Camus, I stumbled over Kierkegaard. Comprehending at first only a sentence here and a paragraph there, I found him a boon companion in my dialogue with Camus. Here was a man as honest as Camus who was asking similar questions, but arriving at different answers. In fact, I argued with them both, because neither of their narratives about the world matched the one in which I had been raised. But both of them offered insights that echoed my own experience and kept me curious.

And for every Twain in my reading, I found a Flannery O'Connor. Satirical, irreverent, and shocking, she taught me that if I didn't have to swallow everything that came cascading over the pulpit, neither need I embrace everything pontificated from lecterns by learned academics. Yes, O'Connor said through her stories, good and evil are real and separate things, and only fools and certain Bible salesmen think otherwise.

Kierkegaard and O'Connor and many others gave me all the license I would need to ask every question, entertain every answer, and still, if I chose, remain somewhere within the galaxy of faith. Their stories—both the ones they lived and the ones they wrote—

became part of my own experience with life, part of the raw material out of which I constructed my own story.

Stories first shape our view of the world and then confirm it. There is something self-fulfilling about stories that is maddening to the Descartes-like rationalist who thinks he or she works only with verifiable givens and leakproof reasoning. I am attracted to certain stories now in part because the stories of my past predispose me to see them as true and powerful. Because the stories of my childhood and youth helped me to believe in good and evil and the responsibility to choose as best I can between them, I continued to be drawn to such stories as an adult.

Not surprisingly, perhaps, the people who most clearly retain those old categories of good and evil are those who have suffered most—at times because of the collapse of the distinction. Never in history have the intellectuals of the world been as dismissive of the categories of good and evil; never has evil more clearly manifested itself in slaughter and oppression. In recent years I have found the most powerful storytellers to be those whose vision has been refined by suffering—survivors of the Holocaust, of totalitarianism, of racism and sexism and all manner of oppression.

Elie Wiesel writes stories of pain filtered through intelligence, yearning, and compassion. In *Night,* his first, highly autobiographical novel, he records the death of an idea of God in the soul of a young boy, himself, in the ovens of Auschwitz. Confronted with the flames of the furnaces and the slaughter of children, the young boy utters a terrible vow of remembrance:

> Never shall I forget that night, the first night in camp, which has turned my life into one long night, seven times cursed and seven times sealed. Never shall I forget that smoke. Never shall I forget the little faces of the children, whose bodies I saw turned into wreaths of smoke beneath a silent blue sky.
>
> Never shall I forget those flames which consumed my faith forever.
>
> Never shall I forget that nocturnal silence which deprived

me, for all eternity, of the desire to live. Never shall I forget those moments which murdered my God and my soul and turned my dreams to dust. Never shall I forget these things, even if I am condemned to live as long as God Himself. Never. (44)

His young protagonist comes to a conclusion that is worse than the death of God—the belief that God exists but is not just.

If _Night_ records a kind of death of God for Wiesel, most of what he has written in the many years since is an accounting of his attempt to reestablish a relationship with God—one that is fair both to his experience and to God. That such a relationship is possible, and yet heartbreakingly difficult, is important to me, someone who has suffered very little and yet shares some of Wiesel's questions.

Though I rightfully say I have suffered very little, it is the very nature and power of story that makes it possible for a few moments for Wiesel's suffering, and that of his characters, to be literally my suffering. The root meaning of compassion is "to suffer with." Stories exist to create compassion for their characters, including their most deformed ones.[1] Though it would be foolish to equate my compassion with Wiesel's original passion (pain), it is hard-hearted and obtuse to deny this ability of story to share and in some mysterious way to alleviate pain. For whatever it is that makes me able to grieve with and for Wiesel's characters in his novel also makes me able to participate in the pain of Mrs. Weingarten—the woman who comes every year to speak to my students of her loss of mother and father, family and friends, and nearly her own life in Auschwitz. It is, in fact, that which makes me able to care about anyone outside myself.

Stories—whether fictional, mythic, historical, or autobiographical—allow me to visualize how certain ways of living might work if I tried them in my own life. They model for me a way I could live or try to live. It does not matter that the characters may not be much like me, or that their circumstances are far removed from mine. For stories to work, it is enough that I am human—and willing to listen.

The stories of suffering and oppression from Wiesel and from others like Solzhenitsyn, Alice Walker, Leslie Silko, Toni Morrison, and Scott Momaday have had one minor effect on me among many important ones. They have cured me of whining—material and existential. My whole scale has changed. I am part of a culture that sees instant gratification as an inalienable right and plunges into fits of self-pity when it is not forthcoming. I take for granted, and even find slightly tedious, fortuitous conditions for making a life about which billions would not dare even dream. Hearing the stories of the writers mentioned above makes it difficult to join the chorus of complaining that currently echoes through our society.

Of course, it serves no purpose to tell others they exaggerate their problems. Such an insight is most useful when turned toward oneself. If my neighbor's angst seems inflated, perhaps it is because I have not listened with the same compassion to his or her story as I did to Wiesel's. But I can judge my own story, and the exposure to these others tells me clearly that the circumstances of my life give me grounds only for gratitude. It is a practical and tangible result of certain stories in my life.

The stories of the oppressed, however, do more than make me grateful for my own good fortune. They also encourage me to act in the world so that others can share in that good fortune. When Martin Luther King says, "I'm just referring to a little history . . ." he makes me want to be part of that history, the history of justice overcoming indifference and hatred through the power of suffering love. Because stories can, in fact, literally give us courage. The child who hears of another child outwitting a giant in a fairy tale is better equipped to conquer the equally fearsome giants in his or her own life. The woman who hears that another has protected herself and her children from an abusive husband, or who has read Alice Walker's *The Color Purple,* is more likely to find the strength to do the same.

This is one of many reasons to reject the flippant response "It's just a story" or the false distinction between stories and "the real world." Stories are more real and more determinative in our lives than the vast majority of things that go on in the merely physical world. Stories form our minds and spirits, the way we perceive ourselves and others, and how we act in the world. Strip the world of story and it becomes more a simple mechanism—and therefore less real.

The stories of our past have a filtering effect that partially determines the stories we will embrace in our present and future. Nonetheless, new and surprising chapters to those stories can be heard or lived for the first time. A fixed set of stories from the past which one constantly replows can be unhealthy if it precludes new realities or new expressions of old themes.

A small but significant addition to my own storehouse of family stories took place a few years ago. I will tell the story in the language of my upbringing, a way of talking that may be foreign to those who grew up differently.

Sometimes we are shaped by characters we never knew existed, and by stories we have never heard. A few years back I was invited to speak at John Brown University in Siloam Springs, Arkansas. I had never heard of John Brown University. Wanting to know a little about the place and people, I asked the chaplain to send me some information on the school.

I discovered that John Brown had been a traveling, southern, tent meeting, sawdust trail evangelist of the early and middle part of the twentieth century. He had traveled along the South, as far west as California, saving the lost and admonishing the saved, and at some point had started a little school.

I will admit to a flicker of condescension when I read this sketch of the school's founder. I am just old enough to have witnessed a sawdust trail tent meeting or two. These are not the Augustines or Pascals of religious faith. I also know something about idiosyncratic institutions which are dominated by the personality of an eccentric founder, sometimes well after that founder has passed on. I did not make any sweeping judgments, but somewhere in the back of my mind I prepared myself for the possibility of a few days in a backwater place with backwater people.

Shortly before leaving for Arkansas, I was talking on the phone with my father. He asked me what I was up to and I mentioned I was going to a place called John Brown University. He replied, "Oh yes, John Brown. Your grandfather Nick was saved under John Brown."

It was one of those moments when God reveals to you in great clarity how stupid you are.

My father then told me a story I had never heard. My grandfather Nick had left a crowded and troubled home in Indiana when he was fifteen or sixteen. It was shortly before World War I and he had nowhere to go, so he jumped on a freight train heading west.

Eventually he ended up in Los Angeles—lonely and without direction. One night he wandered by a revival meeting being led by John Brown. He went in and there he met God. And because he became a Christian, in a personal and life-directing way, he later looked for a Christian woman to marry, and they chose to raise their only child—my father—as a Christian, and he chose a Christian woman to marry, and they chose to raise me and my brothers as believers.

So I discovered that this man, John Brown, whom I had safely pigeonholed as someone far removed from and of no relevance to my life, was in fact an important link in the chain to my own salvation.

It was a story I needed to hear.

One does not have to be sympathetic to Christianity or religious belief or the idea of salvation to understand how a story like this might have some influence on me—on my character—even as an adult. I didn't just hear this story, I accepted it—made it a part of who I was and how I thought about myself and life. It reinforced my sense of living in a coherent universe, of belonging to something important that has stretched over time, of being a link in a chain—indebted to many in the past, mostly unknown to me, and responsible to many in the future, who likewise will not know who I was.

* * *

In the mid-nineteenth century, Matthew Arnold visited the famous monastery at Chartreuse in France. Like so many Victorian intellectuals, Arnold had reluctantly given up Christian faith as the seemingly necessary price for being a modern man. He finds himself unexpectedly moved, however, by the tradition of devotion and faith represented by the monks at Chartreuse, and more than a little envious of the sense of meaning their faith gives them. In the middle of his reverie, as recorded in his poem "Stanzas from the Grand Chartreuse," he suddenly feels the disapproval of his secular mentors who certainly would not commend his emotional indulgence:

> *All are before me! I behold*
> *The House, the Brotherhood austere!*
> *—And what am I, that I am here?*
>
> *For rigorous teachers seized my youth,*
> *And purged its faith, and trimmed its fire,*
> *Showed me the high, white star of Truth,*
> *There bade me gaze, and there aspire.*
> *Even now their whispers pierce the*
> *gloom:*
> What dost thou in this living tomb?
>
> *Forgive me, masters of the mind!*
> *At whose behest I long ago*
> *So much unlearnt, so much resigned—*
> *I come not here to be your foe!*

Though ending up in a different place than Arnold, I believe I know how he felt. I have felt strongly in the past, and on occasion in the present, that I belong to two incompatible worlds. I inherited a stream of stories of faith from my childhood and youth; I later discovered a stream of stories from the world of ideas that is either indifferent or hostile to those founding stories. I heard in my youth a preacher refer scornfully to those with their Ph.D.s (each letter emphasized with great sarcasm) as "educated idiots." I have heard more recently every failing from wife abuse to the thinning ozone layer to logocentric authoritarianism laid at the feet of Christianity. I now straddle these two worlds with a fair degree of equilibrium, but at one point in my life that possibility seemed remote.

What I needed, and what I found, were people to tell me new stories, and to live them out in their own lives. If I was doing more than uncovering a thread through the stories of my life, I would tell of Edward Ericson and Arthur Lynip and others who showed me not only how I could survive the contradictions of my various stories but how I was better for them. But since I cannot tell every story, I will tell the one of Arthur Evans, a man who lived gracefully and serenely at the very place I found myself drowning. I will try to tie down in words something of the role of this remarkable man in my own story:

I want to write this while I think he is still alive.

I saw him last in late fall, a symbolic time in poetry I tell my students. It is one thing they understand immediately, something they feel in their bones.

He was sitting in his wheelchair on the porch of his Atlanta home. His hair was matted in gray swirls, like morning grass where deer have slept. The white stubble of a week's beard spiked his face. A striped robe wrapped haphazardly around his wrinkled cotton pajamas. His head hung down near his chest. He would not have seemed out of place in the senility ward of a decaying home for forgotten people.

Things were not always so.

I first met Dr. Evans in his small office in the Romance Languages building of Emory University. I had waited for him for a year. "Take your language requirement from Dr. Evans," I had been advised. "He likes lit grad students in his class, and he'll let you do your paper in English."

So I waited for him to get back from his sabbatical year in Italy. We stood in his small office and I asked for permission to get into his graduate French class. He was aristocratically gray, slightly built, with a taut carriage that masked his shortness.

"How much French have you studied?"

"I understand it better than I speak it." The familiar lie. "I think I will be able to keep up in the course."

"You're from the English department?"

"Yes. I've finished my course work, but haven't met the language requirement yet."

He looked off into the air, not wanting, it seemed, to make me compromise my integrity any further.

"Well, I am sure that you will learn _something_."

I survived the course, looking attentive while everyone rattled on in French. I did my paper on a passage in Proust—a close New Critical reading that clever English majors can do in their sleep. It was perhaps a nice change of pace for Dr. Evans from pleasant young students who found it easier to speak in two languages than to think in either (a condescending judgment which Dr. Evans would not approve).

Now, however, speaking at all is problematic for Dr. Evans. Parkinson's disease, which first gave him tremors, then brief moments of paralysis, and then took away his legs, has now forbidden him to speak.

He does not obey.

He talks to me on his porch in that late fall meeting, holding up his end of the conversation better than I can mine. Sadly, however, I cannot understand what he is saying. He speaks in a low, rapid mumble. Each word sounds the same to me, like the throaty murmur of an idling motor.

It was not so nearly twenty years ago when, after being mercifully passed in the French class, I sat in on his Dante seminar. He spoke quietly then as well, but with authority and precision. It was the kind of authority that even those who see all authority as exploitation might allow: gentle, not insistent, but, because he was a source of so much light, compelling. He taught like a shy lover, speaking with quiet affection about words he loved.

Now, on his porch, those words were imprisoned in his brain, making breaks for freedom but dying on the inarticulate air, victim of disobedient lip and tongue. I gathered them in but could sift no meaning. I wished his wife Tass would join us. Perhaps she could interpret for me, as those close to the impaired often can. But Tass was on the telephone when I arrived and didn't seem about to get off.

There was no point in pretending to understand. I simply said, "I'm sorry. I do not understand what you are saying." I hoped he would not try again. He immediately tried again.

It was not this way when he first got the disease. I used to see him every year or two, usually in the summer. After graduate school I had moved to Minneapolis, Dr. Evans's boyhood home. Whenever he visited his parents, he would call and we would meet and talk. Once we played tennis together and I entertained him with the story of Ezra Pound's frenetic approach to the game. He later claimed to have mentioned my wicked forehand in a letter of recommendation for one of my futile grant applications (it was characteristic that he would be silent about my backhand).

I both prized and was discomfited by these meetings. Dr. Evans and I were, it seemed to me, from different worlds. He spoke and read many European languages. I spoke native Californian. He wrote monographs about Eastern European writers and scholars whom I had never even seen on a list. I was teaching Baptist kids how to construct a thesis sentence. He was a man of culture and grace. I was the child of an itinerant preacher and truck driver. He was a man in the graying phase of a fine career. I was in the survival phase of a noncareer, trying to do right by wife and children.

We talked of literature and the world. He always inquired about my writing. I always was honest about doing none. He never failed to tell me I should be writing, without leaving any residue of guilt that I wasn't. He made it seem that of course when I got around to writing it would go well, but that, yes, it was certainly acceptable that I wasn't writing at the moment.

Once he came to my house for breakfast. He showed genuine

affection for my children and never failed to ask about each of them individually after that. He thought highly of my wife, which speaks well for both of them.

One year we talked while walking around Lake of the Isles in south Minneapolis. It was the summer of the overthrow of the Shah of Iran. We agreed that it seemed a good thing and that initial complaints about the Ayatollah Khomeini's persecution of enemies seemed exaggerated. Clearly, reading and goodwill do not guarantee political judgment.

That may have been the last time we walked together. He informed me by letter that he had been diagnosed with Parkinson's. The next time we met he looked fine but we did not walk. A year or two after that things were different.

We met at his sister's house. She greeted me at the door. I looked for the same natural dignity in her that was in her older brother and thought I found it. "Art is out back on the patio." She took me through the house and out to a small backyard shaded by large trees. Dr. Evans was seated in a white wrought-iron chair beside a small table on which rested lemonade and cookies. A second chair waited on the other side of the table.

Only later did I realize that he had arranged to be seated and in place when I arrived. He greeted me warmly as always, perhaps more witty and animated even than usual. He inquired about Jayne and the children. We talked about the university and people I had known. We moved on to writers and writing when the first spell of paralysis came on. I think he was in the middle of a sentence about Hemingway in Italy when the words wound down and his face locked. He raised just a finger on his left hand to signal me not to be alarmed. In less than thirty seconds he managed to whisper, "Just a moment. It will pass in a moment." And a few seconds later he finished his comment about Hemingway.

We talked directly about the disease then. He said, among other things, that it might be affected by his personality. He was given to dark periods, he said. It was the first I knew of it. He indicated that psychological profiles of people with Parkinson's showed a correlation with personality types. I don't think he used the word "depression."

I was momentarily preoccupied with this revelation of "dark periods." Where amidst all that learning, all that grace, all that human kindness was there room for darkness of mind and spirit? And where did his tracking after God enter in?

We both were Christians in an out-of-date sense. He was Catholic. I was a mongrel Protestant—heir of as many backwater denominations as would have my father to preach to them for a year or two at a time.

We didn't talk about religion much, but enough to know we were both out of step with our times and our profession. He related that two of Tass's great thrills in life were running unexpectedly into Mother Teresa, once on a plane and again at a hospital. "A moment of blessing" was how he put it, I think. I tried to tell him something of life among the fundamentalists and he seemed to understand.

I didn't know exactly what Dr. Evans believed or how, but I was sure it was thoughtful, and gentle, and, what shall I say, profound. And I'm sure it had something to offer him for those dark periods, but not anything that would explain them away. Maybe it was dark periods that started him feeling for transcendence in the first place.

We had only infrequent contact between visits, usually in the form of a card from him or a short letter from me. His cards would often bear only a citation of an interesting article: "See TLS 21 March 1977 for nice piece on Wyndham Lewis," and on one occasion two taped Karl Barth stamps. As the disease progressed the handwriting on the cards degenerated. The last had only two words, declining precipitously toward the bottom of the card. As best I could figure out, they said, "miss you."

And now here I was in the late fall sitting in Atlanta on the porch of this man whose body had almost completely abandoned him. I was uncomfortable but determined to be natural, to do what a friend would do for a friend in this situation, even a friend a generation older whom one knew only incompletely.

I tried carrying the conversation by myself, to tell what I was up to these days, how Jayne and the children were, what books I had been reading. But all this filled only a few minutes at best and I was left scratching for words to overcome the silence. I hadn't the courage to be quiet, nor the heart to keep repeating, "I do not understand"—knowing that this only prompted him to try again.

I decided this must be painful for him and concluded I should leave. I felt profoundly sad. This was an incredible waste. Dr. Evans should be at the peak of his powers. He should have ten years before retirement to plow whatever fields of thought he wants to plow and then ten or twenty more years enjoying his grandchildren and books and art museums and Italy.

Moreover, we are losing, I thought, a gentleman scholar of a kind often joked about but whose value we are only beginning to recognize as they disappear. He is, in one sense only, like the sisters whom Gabriel Conroy toasts in "The Dead" as practitioners of a now unfashionable graciousness in a contentious and "thought tormented" age. He is not to be sentimentalized like Joyce's maiden aunts, but the widespread loss of such civility and humaneness should be more lamented than it is.

But civility and humaneness are insufficient words. These are the prized and disappearing qualities that allow us to talk together profitably about things that divide us. There seems little room for them in a world where so many people preface their assertions with the formula "I am outraged." But important as they are, these are not adequate to describe Dr. Evans. His is graciousness in the theological sense—the showing of unmerited favor, seeing and treating people as better than they deserve, as God treats us. If we have ever experienced such grace, we know its transforming power.

As I rose to leave that afternoon, Dr. Evans spoke once more. I leaned forward, determined to understand at least something before I went.

"i mm eadim or n pees."

"I'm sorry. I didn't understand."

"i mm eadin wor n pece."

"_War and Peace?_"

"I mm reademm war un peace."

He was reading *War and Peace*.

I was greatly moved and humbled. Even though I knew that the disease had attacked his brain, not his mind, I had somehow drifted into accepting that his physical appearance was a partial index to his mental life.

Such a mistake was an insult to our relationship and to my knowledge of him. The slow extinguishing of the body did not prevent him from nursing the fires of the mind. He was not raging against the dying of the light so much as tending his own beacon. This was, in every crucial respect, still the man who had pretended to believe I understood French so many years before.

When I announced my departure, Dr. Evans protested that I had just gotten there, which was true. But I had already stood to go, and I feared my staying only brought him frustration. I knew another former student was due in a few minutes. And I knew also that part of me wanted to escape the pain of being helpless to release an extraordinary man from his lot.

As I walked down the porch, leaving Dr. Evans in his wheelchair, I looked in the window at Tass as she spoke on the phone. I thought she gave me a reproachful look, perhaps only the projection of my own troubled spirit. Six months later I called Dr. Evans's son, knowing that my friend could not himself be understood on the phone. He told me Tass had died of cancer. Dr. Evans was weaker. It didn't seem fair.

It has been over a year now and I haven't called again. I tell myself at least once a week I am going to call. Maybe I will as soon as I finish writing this. Yes, I will definitely call.

Of course, the reason I do not is that I am afraid to hear that Dr. Evans has died. I know when that happens the world will be diminished and so will I. And I know I will feel guilty.

But why so gloomy? Perhaps he is still fighting the good fight. Perhaps I'll find that he is reading, in Italian, the *Paradiso*.

※ ※ ※

Arthur Evans died last year. His sister, echoing his thoughtful-ness, called to tell me. I don't know that he got around to reading the *Paradiso,* but I like to believe he is now experiencing it firsthand. If that is a foolish belief, it is one we shared together, and I am happy to hold up my end in his absence.

So John Brown and Dr. Evans take their places—along with Stephen the Martyr, Augustine, Pascal, Thoreau, Melville, Kierke-gaard, Tolstoy, Camus, King, Koufax and Drysdale, Phyllis, Huck, and so many others—in the account of that small part of me that believes in good and evil. It is a strange mix, maybe even eccentric in the present age, but it is mine and of course I prize it. These characters and their stories have shaped who I am and how I live in the world. No wonder I will not give them up easily. Any competing and contradictory stories will have to be very powerful indeed for me to embrace them, not only compelling in their own right but desta-bilizing to my own.

We are all wedded to our stories. It doesn't mean we are each hermetically sealed in our own little worlds, impervious to the influ-ence of others. It does mean the only way to avoid such isolation is to listen, compassionately, to the stories of others.

6

Healing Broken Stories

*If I don't tell someone, I'm not sure what will happen.
I'll crack perhaps.*

Jane Augustine

In remembrance lies the secret of redemption.

Baal Shem-Tov

Stories can be broken. The stories we live by sometimes fall apart.
They no longer adequately explain our experience or give us enough
reason to get up in the morning. Even worse, we sometimes come to
doubt there is any story to our lives at all. They seem plotless. We
lose any sense of ourselves as characters making significant choices.
We cannot imagine a meaningful outcome to events. In such cases
we need to heal our broken stories. The best cure for a broken story
is another story.

No story has been more relentlessly battered than that of the
Jews. They have survived as a people only because of their commit-
ment to storytelling. Elie Wiesel prefaces his novel *The Gates to the
Forest* with the following brief story:

> When the great Rabbi Israel Baal Shem-Tov saw misfortune
> threatening the Jews it was his custom to go into a certain part
> of the forest to meditate. There he would light a fire, say a
> special prayer, and the miracle would be accomplished and the
> misfortune averted.

Later, when his disciple, the celebrated Magid of Mezritch, had occasion, for the same reason, to intercede with heaven, he would go to the same place in the forest and say: "Master of the universe, listen! I do not know how to light the fire, but I am still able to say the prayer." And again the miracle would be accomplished.

Still later, Rabbi Moshe-Leib of Sasov, in order to save his people once more, would go into the forest and say: "I do not know how to light the fire, I do not know the prayer, but I know the place and this must be sufficient." It was sufficient and the miracle was accomplished.

Then it fell to Rabbi Israel of Rizhyn to overcome misfortune. Sitting in his armchair, his head in his hands, he spoke to God: "I am unable to light the fire and I do not know the prayer; I cannot even find the place in the forest. All I can do is to tell the story, and this must be sufficient." And it was sufficient.

God made man because he loves stories.

Wiesel's novel, set during the Holocaust, that most demonic annihilator of stories, itself tries to preserve a fragment of the story. When our lives are most shattered, and we no longer know the first letter of the alphabet, we do well to recall our stories—or to embrace new ones.

The right stories can heal our brokenness and cure what ails us. They do so most often by reconnecting us with others who share our story, rescuing us from the sterile cycle of self-absorption, alienation, and radical skepticism. When our own ability to narrate our story falters, we can lean on the shared story to sustain us.

Every story implies a community, and community offers us our single best hope for healing broken stories. At its smallest a story defines a community of two: teller and listener. At its largest, it embraces the entire human community and beyond. Whether small or large, community is healing because it both requires something of us and gives us something back. In story, both teller and listener have responsibilities to the other, responsibility being the fair price we pay for the many benefits of sharing a story with others.

This reciprocal responsibility inhabits both stories in books and in our lives, the boundary between the two being more fluid than we often realize. Anything valuable we can say about the nature of story in literature is likely to be true also of those we share together in our communities. In both cases, it is only the story that affects how we actually live that is significant.

Most advice to storytellers focuses on the craft of telling or the relation of the teller to the tale; too little attention is paid to the responsibility of the teller to the audience. We should think more about what is _right_ for the teller to do, not just what is effective. A very old but currently suspect notion (especially in sophisticated circles) is that a story should be told so as to benefit the audience. It is very old because stories first arose in communities, and why would someone want to tell a story that harmed the community or wasted its time? It is unpopular today because we have deified the isolated individual and see any expectation of responsibility of the individual storyteller to the group as limiting and threatening.

Martin Marty tells a story of Martin Buber telling a story about a rabbi who told a story about how his grandfather had told a story illustrating how stories are to be told: "So Buber told a story about a rabbi whose grandfather had been a pupil of the great founder of Hasidism, Baal Shem Tov. This rabbi was once asked to tell a story. 'A story ought to be told so that it is itself a help,' and his story was as follows: 'My grandfather was paralyzed. Once he was asked to tell a story about his teacher and he told how the holy Baal Shem-Tov used to jump and dance when he was praying. My grandfather stood up while he was telling the story and the story carried him away so much that he had to jump and dance to show how the master had done it. From that moment, he was healed. This is how stories ought to be told" (142).

Yes, this is how stories ought to be told: with passion and belief and abandonment—with our entire selves. It is how every great community storyteller—from Moses to Malcolm X—*has* narrated the community story. And it is worth noting that this story about the rabbi came through many hands to Buber and then to Marty and then to me by way of a colleague who had read other stories in a book of mine and thought I would profit from hearing this story. And now I am telling it to you. This is the way with good and healing stories—we want to share them with others.

Such shared stories define a community and offer us healing. More than the color of skin, or shared ideas, or gender, or social class, it is stories held and valued in common that tie us to each other. Any movement—political, religious, ideological—that does not have the power through its shared story to unite people from widely divergent backgrounds is doomed. Even families are united more by mutual stories—of love and pain and adventure—than by biology. "Do you remember when . . ." bonds people together far more than shared chromosomes. Stories are thicker than blood.

Buber's dancing paralytic told a story he believed in and it healed him. His story took him out of himself. What seemed an inevitable and unchangeable reality was changed for a new reality because his identification with another through story enabled him to transcend the limitations of the isolated self. He believed the story he told and that belief changed reality.

What does it mean to *believe* the story you are telling? It means, among many things, that you believe it is true—even if it is about hobbits or events that could never happen. True does not mean factual (though it may be factual); true means accurately reflecting human experience. (Being human, storytellers can only witness to the human experience, even if it is the human experience of the nonhuman.) In the presence of a true story we say, "Yes, this is how it feels; this is how it would happen; this is what one might think."

Believing one's own story also means believing that it is worth telling—both for oneself and for one's audience. The most precious commodity each of us possesses is time. Thoreau told us that we should gauge the cost of things not by dollars but by the amount of our lives we spend to buy them. Stories are an accounting of lives spent—well spent and wasted—and we, in turn, spend our lives in listening to and living them. Tellers of stories ought to believe we are better for having heard their stories. Those who do not believe in the value of their own stories are wasting their lives and ours.

The storyteller also has the obligation to tell the story so it can be understood—though not necessarily by everyone. The community for which the story is told determines the language of the story. The more committed to the welfare of the community the storyteller is, the more he or she takes the language and experience of the community as raw material for the story.

Quincy Troupe, for example, consciously writes for an African-American community that understands a man who spends his life killing animals in a slaughterhouse and what it might do to him:

> big tom was a black nigga man
> cold & black
> eye say, big tom was a black nigga man
> black steel flesh
> standin like a gladiator
> soaked in animal blood, bits of flesh
> wringin wet
> standin at the center of death
> buzzard hoverin
> swingin his hamma named death
> 260 workdays
> swingin his hamma named death (76)

The story of this man's dehumanization, symbolic of the dehumanization threatening the entire community, is literally good for that community. Through sensuous detail, repetition, and rhythm the poem creates a character (in this case re-creates an actual character) and a setting and an action that its intended audience understands. And that audience also understands that life can equally well rob them of their own humanity, especially if they allow themselves, like this man, to be cut off from the community.

Troupe could not, I believe, be a poet on the printed page alone. He frequently reads—performs—his poems in person: in classrooms, bars, and prisons (Moyers). In keeping with the oral tradition in which all stories began, he creates a relationship with his audience that encourages and energizes them both.

Sometimes what we need most is simply to laugh and celebrate ourselves. In a poem describing the amazing exploits of the great Magic Johnson, Troupe celebrates with his community the heroics of a wondrous athlete they feel is one of their own. His poem allows all lovers of basketball to participate, but only if they will adapt to the language of the community. The poem ends as follows:

> *in victory we suddenly sense your glorious uplift*
> *your urgent need to be champion*
> *& so we cheer, rejoicing with you for this quicksilver,*
>   *quicksilver, quicksilver*
> *moment of fame, so put the ball on the floor again, "magic"*
> *juke & dazzle, shaking & baking down the lane*
> *take the sucker to the hoop, "magic" johnson*
> *recreate reverse hoodoo gems off the spin*
> *deal alley-oop-dunk-a-thon-magician passes, now*
> *double-pump, scissor, vamp through space, hang in place*
> *& put it all in the sucker's face, "magic" johnson*
> *& deal the roundball like the juju man that you am*
> *like the sho-nuff shaman man that you am*
> *"magic," like the shonuff spaceman you am* (117)

And if you think you now know this poem, you are wrong. Because you have not fully experienced the poem until you have been part of a crowd (a community) for which Troupe has performed the poem. When you see the energy and joy that passes back and forth between them, you understand something of the binding power of shared stories.

That these poetic stories may be less accessible or impressive to some outside Quincy Troupe's community is not a problem. Every community tells its own stories. Some are for the community only, and others travel far beyond (because among all our communities we share the common bond of being human). Some stories are for everyone; others are for only one other person. But even the most complex and experimental stories must care that someone understand them. They should be difficult not because the teller cultivates obscurity, but because some things cannot be said simply.

Storytellers should be aware that they are dealing with dangerous materials. Life and death flow to us through stories. Words have almost unlimited power to destroy and to heal. Nothing is more false than the implication of the phrase "Words, words, words— nothing but words." More lives have been destroyed by words than by bullets, and more lives redeemed and made whole.

Writers and storytellers are responsible not to poison the lives of their hearers with toxic stories. If stories have the power to enlighten and heal us, they must, by definition, have the power to mislead and harm us. Nazi Germany told itself powerful and compelling stories, but they were stories of death. If our storytellers fail us, the people perish.

If storytellers have responsibilities, so do their audiences. We should attend not only to how stories are told, but also to how they are received. Listening is an ethical task.

Our first obligation as receivers of stories is that we do in fact listen. Everyone, without exception, has the right to tell his or her own story. We are not obligated to approve that person's story, but we are obligated to hear it. Too often in human history this basic right has been denied. A primary instrument of oppression is silencing. Specific methods include denying a people their language, the ability to read and write, a knowledge of their history, a forum to articulate their grievances and aspirations, and so on.

Ignazio Silone had this in mind when he tried to give voices to Italian peasants in novels like _Fontamara_ and _Bread and Wine_. In the foreword to _Fontamara_ he stated this first principle of listening in the simplest terms: "Let everyone, then, have the right to tell his story in his own way" (20). This is the minimum we owe every human being, and crucial to any hope we have for getting along in a society made up of many cultures and varied commitments.

How we listen is also important. If we are to receive the stories we need, we must listen well. In the opening to *Their Eyes Were Watching God,* Zora Neale Hurston depicts her central character, Janie, returning to town after a long period of rich and painful living, "full of that oldest human longing—self revelation" (6). She needs to tell someone what has happened to her and to those she loved. Although everyone in town is interested—in the way we are interested in looking at a wreck alongside the road—only her friend Pheoby is interested in Janie as well as in her story. It is to Pheoby, then, that she unburdens herself, and, Hurston tells us, "Pheoby's hungry listening helped Janie to tell her story" (10).

With important stories, only "hungry listening" will do. Indifference or detachment is worse than forbidding the story outright. It dehumanizes this most human of activities: "Here is what happened to me. What do you think? What happened to you?"

The last question is crucial. Community is formed only by *shared* stories, not by monologues. Empathetic listening is followed, in time, by reciprocal storytelling. I know I have a place in the community not only as I hear and accept its stories but as it hears and makes room for mine. (Think again of the invitation in Frost's poem: "You come too.")

This sharing of stories not only preserves valuable experiences of the past, the recountings are themselves fresh experiences. Martin Marty, citing Buber, says, "The story is itself an event and has the quality of a sacred action. . . . It is more than a reflection—the sacred essence to which it bears witness continues to live in it. The wonder that is narrated becomes powerful once more" (Marty 142). Storytelling works in conjunction with memory and imagination to give new or continued life to the emotions, ideas, and experiences of the past. They are not so much recalled as they are relived, experienced again, telling after telling. How else can we explain being moved nearly 3,000 years later by Hector's death, or the fresh anger and desire for revenge that accompanies the telling of ancient tales of injustice in Ireland, the Balkans, or the Middle East?

William Wordsworth's famous description of the composition of poetry as "the spontaneous overflow of powerful feelings" (740) applies also to storytelling and listening. Wordsworth claims that poetry is created "from emotion recollected in tranquillity." He makes clear that although the recollection may begin "in tranquillity," the remembered events soon produce new and present emotions that are siblings to the remembered ones. The feelings are not simply remembered; they are experienced again. Stories entangle in words and rhythms the power of the original experiences, making possible the release of that power wherever the words are spoken once more.

This power of stories derives in part from their partaking in the character of ritual. Rituals are those things we do over and over again. Meaningful rituals are things we repeatedly do *voluntarily* because we find them helpful or comforting. Sacred rituals are those that tie us somehow to the transcendent, to everlasting things that are larger than ourselves.

Human beings always have been and always will be creatures of ritual. There is something comforting in chosen repetition. As was suggested earlier, it may begin as early as the unborn child's familiarity with the mother's heartbeat. It is reinforced by the rhythms of day and night, and of the seasons. At its most fundamental, ritual is a vote against chaos and randomness and arbitrary death.

When we perform a ritual, and *perform* is the key word, we know for that time at least what we are doing in life. "This is what should be done, and then this. And this is how to do it." Such knowledge is an encouragement and protection against those other times when we are less sure we know what we are doing or what is going to happen to us.

It is no accident that significant rituals almost always tell stories.

"Why is this night different from all other nights?" So asks the child during the Jewish Passover celebration, and the question demands a story for its answer. "On the night in which our Lord was betrayed, he took a cup . . ." So begins the ritual of Christian communion. "Oh, say, can you see . . ." begins the national anthem, a story we for some reason feel it appropriate to tell before countless sporting events.

Stories participate in the character of rituals in many ways. They weave the experiences of life into apprehendable patterns. Depending on how skeptical one is, stories either reveal the underlying connectedness of things or give us the illusion of connectedness in a random world.

Stories, like rituals, are repeated, gaining power from each re-telling. Children often request a story with the words "Tell me the one about . . ." and younger children frequently insist that every word be the same as before. Their pleasure in the retelling of the familiar story is not unlike the pleasure and reassurance in the thousandth taking of the bread and wine, or passing of the unleav-ened bread, or bowing in the direction of Mecca—or listening again, in the ritual of theater, to King Lear's final speech with his dead daughter in his arms.

And like ritual, stories create and bond together a community. They draw us together to share in the ritual of telling—spiritually together if we are reading a book, spiritually and physically if we are witnessing a play or worshiping together or sharing a story between friends. And in the shared telling we find—as in ritual—beauty and truth and mystery and, sometimes, goodness. We go away from such experiences better equipped for life.

No one understands this link between ritual, story, and health better than those cultures that have had their stories ravaged. Leslie Marmon Silko embodies the kaleidoscope of cultures that is the Americas, herself Laguna Pueblo, Mexican, and white. Raised on a reservation near Albuquerque, she has witnessed the effects on Native Americans of broken stories. Silko tells of one such broken story, and the struggle to heal it, in her novel _Ceremony_. The words that preface the novel parallel Wiesel's invocation of past Hasidic masters cited earlier:

I will tell you something about stories . . .
They aren't just entertainment.
Don't be fooled.
They are all we have, you see,
all we have to fight off
illness and death.

You don't have anything
if you don't have the stories.

Their evil is mighty
but it can't stand up to our stories.
So they try to destroy the stories
let the stories be confused or forgotten.
They would like that
They would be happy
Because we would be defenseless then.

He rubbed his belly.
I keep them here . . .
Here, put your hand on it
See, it is moving.
There is life here
for the people.

And in the belly of this story
the rituals and the ceremony
are still growing.

When the stories of an individual or a culture fall apart, both are defenseless. Without our stories we literally do not know who we are or what we should do. The last words before the beginning of Silko's novel offer a prescription for what ails her culture, and perhaps most of us:

> *The only cure*
> *I know*
> *is a good ceremony . . .*

Her story which follows is itself a kind of ceremony, and in it lies healing.

One of the most encouraging truths in a difficult world is that we have the freedom to change our defining stories. Broken stories can be restored, deficient ones replaced, and healthy stories identified and nurtured. If many of our stories are inherited from the various communities of which we are a part, they are also chosen and lived. We can be active participants, not merely passive receivers, in the making and remaking of our story.

Broken or diseased stories are those that fail in any of the crucial areas in which a life story must succeed. They give an inadequate sense of plottedness and meaning to our lives, or of ourselves as characters. Failed stories tend to ignore or undervalue either our freedom or our responsibility. They bind us to explanations of the world that do not correspond with our own experience, or they leave us isolated in a desperate pursuit of individual satisfaction like a dog chasing its tail.

Healing broken stories requires our active participation. The only stories that will be significant for us in the long run are those we help tell ourselves. Literary criticism has recently begun to emphasize the degree to which readers participate in the creation of the story they read. Readers must agree to participate in the imaginative world of the story in the first place, to suspend the part of the brain that says, "You are sitting in your tattered chair in your heavily mortgaged living room and your marriage is more than a little shaky. This is reality. The book you are holding is just a bunch of words."

Beyond this fundamental expression of sympathy for the text, the reader also fills in endless details of atmosphere in the story, visualizing characters and action and motivation in more detail than the writer can possibly provide. Most stories written in the last hundred years welcome this reader participation, and may even make the reader more responsible for evaluating actions and motivations than is comfortable (for instance, by having multiple narrators giving different versions of the same events, none of them totally reliable).

As we participate in creating the stories we read, so should we participate in the creation of the stories by which we live. Although every story we hear has the power to affect us, a handful of core stories determine the general shape of our lives. These are the stories that most directly answer the big questions: who am I, why am I here, who are these others, what is success, what should I do, what will happen when I die? These are our life stories, the ones that organize reality for us, give us our values, and enable us to explain our experience.

We should evaluate these core stories by the highest criteria and act accordingly if they are found wanting. We can heal our stories and choose new ones, for instance, by becoming true, acting characters rather than mere personalities. Characters are defined by their choices, and their choices are a reflection of their values and understanding of the world. Your most meaningful stories should be chosen, not lived by default.

Many times the stories you choose _will_ be the ones that come from the communities in which you live. There is no particular merit or benefit in rejecting a story simply because it is familiar. But in choosing such stories, rather than passively receiving them, they become _your_ story, and the community story will be different because you are a part of it.

Sometimes, however, our stories are not merely broken or fragmented, they are profoundly flawed. They cannot be healed, only replaced. The same freedom and responsibility that make us characters, also give us the possibility of choosing new stories in which to live. One of the clearest indications of a flawed life story is its failure to give one the sense of purpose and conviction necessary to live life with an acceptable degree of optimism and resolve. A failed story no longer encourages the kind of life you feel it is important to live.

Stories can fail on every level from the cosmic to the intensely private. We looked in the previous chapter at Augustine abandoning a series of failed stories by which he tried to live his life for the story of Christ. And of course just as many have changed their stories to align with defining stories of faith, so others have moved away from these stories to ones they judge more fitting to their experience and aspirations.

The movement in either direction is often revolutionary, entailing a whole new way of seeing reality and acting in it. Stephen Crites describes the reorientation that takes place when one changes the central story by which one understands life: "The stories within which he has awakened to consciousness must be undermined, and in the identification of his personal story through a new story both the drama of his experience and his style of action must be reoriented. Conversion is reawakening, a second awakening of consciousness. His style must change steps, he must dance to a new rhythm. Not only his past and future, but the very cosmos in which he lives is strung in a new way" (307).

The poet Adrienne Rich, for example, explains her movement to feminism as a long process during which the explanations of the world with which she grew up and by which she tried to live proved increasingly untenable to her. She describes the "pain and confusion of that inward wrenching of the self" when one's fundamental stories are called into question (245). Rich looked to other storytellers to help her construct a new story for herself: "I began searching for some clue or key to life, not only in poetry but in political writers. The writers I found were Mary Wollstonecraft, Simone de Beauvoir, and James Baldwin. Each of them helped me to realize that what had seemed simply 'the way things are' could actually be a social construct, advantageous to some people and detrimental to others, and that these constructs could be criticized and changed."

The realization that things can be other than they are is at the heart of all revolutions and conversions. Rich needed to discover the shared vision of others to understand that the disjunction she felt between her experience and the myths she was living by was not

merely idiosyncratic: "They were not simply part of my private tur-
moil, a secret misery, an individual failure."

Rich also discovered in her mentors a warning about the possible
consequences of changing a life story. She cites James Baldwin's
words: "Any real change implies the breakup of the world as one has
always known it, the loss of all that gave one an identity, the end of
safety." We cling even to broken stories precisely because they are
the only stories we know, or the only ones we can imagine ourselves
living. It feels safer to accept the pain with which we are familiar
than to risk the unknown pain that may be part of change. Rich
testifies to the consolation of community and shared stories when
she says of Baldwin's words, "I don't know why I found these words
encouraging—perhaps because they made me feel less alone."

Or consider Scott Momaday's description of the change that took
place in his mother when she began consciously to identify herself
as a Native American:

> In 1929 my mother was a Southern belle; she was about to
> embark upon an extraordinary life. It was about this time that
> she began to see herself as an Indian. That dim native heritage
> became a fascination and a cause for her, inasmuch, perhaps, as
> it enabled her to assume an attitude of defiance, an attitude
> which she assumed with particular style and satisfaction; it be-
> came her. She imagined who she was. This act of the
> imagination was, I believe, among the most important events of
> my mother's early life, as later the same essential act was to be
> among the most important of my own. (23–24)

New stories lead to new actions and new actions to new stories.
When we envision our lives differently, we are capable of being
different. MacIntyre observes that an "action is always an episode in
a possible history" (216). Every action implies a story because an act
is a choice made by a character in a context. When we fully grasp
both our freedom and our responsibility we can recapture the health
of our past stories or purpose to live in new ones.

This suggests a model for personal and community healing that would often bypass the psychiatrist's couch or the obsessive intro-spection of most therapy. "Finding myself" is less a matter of uncovering some supposedly pristine and genuine self within, one uncorrupted by outside influences, than it is discovering my role in various stories in which I am only one of many characters. Being one character out of many in a larger story does not diminish me; it enlarges me and my possible significance. I am not an isolated individual desperately searching for an illusory self and plaintively insisting on my needs and rights; rather I am a character in a story with other characters, making choices together that give our lives meaning.

All stories, however, are not equal. The relativism that permeates the air we breathe would have us believe that all stories are equally valuable and that no story can be truer than another. This is contra-dicted both by common sense and by common experience. It matters greatly, perhaps eternally, which stories we choose, espe-cially which life stories.

The life stories by which we live should have certain qualities. They can be enumerated in a wide variety of terms. Bettelheim says the following about the requirements for a fairy tale that will prove helpful to a child:

> To enrich his life, it must stimulate his imagination; help him to develop his intellect and to clarify his emotions; be attuned to his anxieties and aspirations; give full recognition to his difficul-ties, while at the same time suggesting solutions to the problems which perturb him. In short, it must at one and the same time relate to all aspects of his personality—and this without ever belittling but, on the contrary, giving full credence to the seri-ousness of the child's predicament, while simultaneously promoting confidence in himself and in his future. (5)

These should be qualities in our stories not only as children but throughout our lives.

Healthy life stories do full justice to our situation, our needs, and our nature. They have many qualities, but I would like to suggest four that should mark the stories in which we choose to act as characters. These stories should be truthful, freeing, gracious, and hopeful.

Good stories often tell us things that never happened, but they never tell us lies. They sometimes use distortion as a strategy, but they are always the enemy of distortion. Joseph Conrad said, "My task which I am trying to achieve is, by the power of the written word to make you hear, to make you feel—it is, before all, to make you _see_" (19). What we _see_ is the world and ourselves more accurately, with a clarity that is helpful for living. And the test is the nature of the life lived.

A true life story explains the world to us in a way that accounts for the facts of our experience. Inadequate stories require constant stretching, patching, deflecting, and suppression. Procrustes is a character from Greek mythology who was less than a perfect host. He invited guests to sleep in a bed but insisted that they fit it perfectly. Anyone who was too short was stretched and made to fit, and anyone too long had overhanging limbs chopped off. Many of us try to live by Procrustean stories that force us to stretch and chop our experience to make it fit.

A truthful life story, as we saw in the last chapter, will not only convincingly account for the facts of our experience, it will be satisfying. It will meet our emotional and intellectual need for meaning and purpose and the sense that our lives have value.

Satisfying, however, is not the same as happy. This is one of the distortions in the common American story of success, a good example of a flawed story that at least needs to be supplemented, if not replaced. Enshrined in our "Declaration of Independence" is the quintessentially American idea that we have the inalienable right to pursue happiness. Originally that probably did not mean much more than the right to private ownership of property (apparently a key to happiness for Americans then as now). But over the years we have subtly modified that idea into not simply the right to pursue happiness but the unquestionable right to *be* happy, which is not the same.

The American success story tells us we are to achieve this happiness primarily through four avenues: money, power, prestige, and pleasure. These are the great themes of countless stories paraded before us in novels, films, self-help books, talk shows, television, and advertising. You can be richer, stronger, sexier. You can be envied, on top, out front, desired. You can be confident, gratified, in control, calling the shots, in charge. And, it goes without saying, you will be happy.

Then why aren't we? Why is arguably the richest, most powerful, most envied, most pleasure-soaked society in human history so widely unhappy? We are filled with complaint, frustration, anxiety, hostility, and violence. At least that is what we tell ourselves through the media day after day. (When was the last time you saw a "study" of anything that concluded that we were healthy and doing well?)

We are unhappy because we are trying to live by a broken story. As attractive as it is in many respects, the American success story simply doesn't tell us the truth. It lies both in suggesting that everyone who works hard enough will have these things and in suggesting that once you have them you will finally be happy. It is a testimony to the human appetite for illusion that this story persists in the face of countless counter-stories from disappointed individuals who have followed these paths and found no contentment.

A satisfying story is one that is true not only to how the world is on the outside but to how we are inside. It is emotionally and spiritually true. We do not have to divide ourselves to live it. We do not have to suppress something we know in our emotions to be true. Such emotional congruence is not a sufficient test by itself, because we know our emotions can support lies, but it is a necessary test. Our spirits will approve our most important stories.

A healthy story is also freeing. Stories that are true conform to reality. Understanding what is real and acting in accordance with it results in freedom—especially the freedom to do things. A bird can fly because it behaves in consort with the aerodynamic laws of nature. It is most free, and most capable, when it aligns itself with the unbreakable laws of how things are. A bird does not lament the restrictive laws of physics; it uses them to soar.

Human beings on the other hand too often think they're flying when they're only falling (Berry 141). Our prevailing notion of freedom is "No one can tell me what to do," when it should more often be "Will someone please tell me what to do?" A life story cut off from the stories of others is likely to be both untrue and sterile. Healthy stories free us from excessive self-absorption and "I did it my way" self-centeredness.

Healthy stories free us both from the lies we tell ourselves and from the lies others tell about us. In Alice Walker's *The Color Purple*, Celie is told, directly and indirectly, that she can never be more than a servant to an abusive husband because she is black, female, friendless, stupid, and ugly. It is a story she believes until another character, Shug, tells her a different story about herself. Braced up by this new story, Celie sees herself and the world differently, acts differently, and thereby changes her world.

Meaningful freedom is not freedom *from* something but freedom to *do* something (Barth 79). Broken stories trap us in repetitive, destructive acts—or make us passive; healthy ones free us to change ourselves and the world. The latter encourage us to see ourselves as characters with meaningful choices, and motivate us to act accordingly. Nothing is more energizing than the feeling that one has something important to do. Nothing is more enervating than the feeling that nothing is worth doing.

One test, then, of our life story is whether it frees and motivates us to act. It should create for us a world where meaning is possible and we have a role in bringing it about. Healthy stories are the enemies of passivity, paralysis, and cynicism. What, specifically, we do as a result of this freedom is unpredictable. It is more likely to be something small than something big. Celie expressed her new freedom by, among other things, designing pants for her friends. Most significant acts in the world are small ones. It is the accumulation of small acts, in individuals and in communities, that changes reality.

Another mark of healthy life stories is grace. Grace is getting better than you deserve—or giving better. Grace breaks the one-to-one link between performance and reward. It is essentially a religious idea, growing out of the notion of a creator with a parent's love for the creation. But it can be a powerful force in anyone's life.

Sacred writings are filled with stories of grace. In the Bible, David refuses the opportunity to kill Saul, the man who is trying to kill him; the forgiving father welcomes back the prodigal son; Christ on the cross prays for forgiveness for his crucifiers. The Bible's central story, in fact, is the story of grace. (See, for instance, Romans 5:8: "But God proved his own love for us by sending Christ to die for us while we were still sinners.")

Even those who no longer look to transcendence for grace often recognize that we cannot live well without it. Raymond Carver, the celebrated short story writer, frequently explores the mysterious operation of grace in his thoroughly secular stories. The gestures of grace may be as unassuming as a good-luck kiss from an ex-chimney sweep in "Where I'm Calling From," or the sitting together of bereaved parents and a baker over hot bread and coffee in "A Small, Good Thing." In the latter story, a woman orders a birthday cake from a thick-necked, coarsed-featured baker for her son's eighth birthday. The baker is abrupt and unfriendly and she feels uncomfortable. On the day of his birthday the boy is hit by a car and is hospitalized. It seems he will be fine once he awakens, but he does not awaken and the parents grow increasingly anxious. Meantime the baker, angry that they have not claimed the cake, begins making anonymous calls to the home. He alludes to the cake indirectly, but does not identify himself. Sometimes he says nothing and simply hangs up after they have answered. The parents, having forgotten about the cake, find the calls mysterious and frightening. The boy suddenly dies. When the baker calls again the mother shouts at him that he is an evil man.

Later it occurs to her who the caller is. She has her husband drive her down to the bakery late at night. She confronts the baker with what he has done, and feels the power of righteous anger. He picks up a rolling pin in case they attack him, but then a strange turn occurs. She tells him that their son is dead, and then begins to cry. The baker puts down his rolling pin, slowly shakes his head, and then invites them to sit down. Mutual anger and mistrust turns to shared grief as the baker apologizes for what he's done. He offers them coffee and hot rolls from his oven, and then tells them some of his own story: "Then he began to talk. They listened carefully. Although they were tired and in anguish, they listened to what the baker had to say. They nodded when the baker began to speak of loneliness, and of the sense of doubt and limitation that had come to him in his middle years. He told them what it was like to be childless all these years" (405).

Sharing stories bridges the gap between them. Their nod of understanding is a gesture of shared humanity and suffering that dissolves their differences, or at least renders them insignificant. The baker's offering of bread and coffee is a secular version of Christian communion. It is the universal ritual of shared food as a sign of hospitality and community. No wonder then that the last lines of the story tell us, "They talked on into the early morning, the high, pale cast of light in the windows, and they did not think of leaving." Shared stories are not easily walked away from.

The giving and receiving of grace should be part of any healthy life story. It is intimately linked to those other qualities of healthy stories—truth and freedom. If the stories I live by are unfettered with falsehood, and if they free me from preoccupation with self so I can act in the world, then I am more likely to be a source of grace to others and, therefore, to receive grace from others.

Grace is the ultimate act of empathy. It is possible on the human level only to the degree that we can imagine ourselves in other people's shoes. Such an act of imagination is a story act. It is being able to see oneself as a character in another's story, and acting in accordance with that imaginative perception in one's own. Grace is more than empathy, but empathy is its starting point. Because I know keenly my own need for receiving better than I deserve, I can imagine your similar need and can use my freedom to fulfill that need.

Grace is therefore a communal act. Only as we feel connected to others will grace flow back and forth. Even the simple, everyday orthodoxies of conversation—"I know how you feel," "That must have hurt," "I would have done the same thing," the nod of the head—are formulas of empathy that may contain flashes of grace.

The opposite of stories of grace are those of hate, revenge, and unrelieved victimhood. Individuals and communities who define themselves primarily in terms of wrongs done to them are unlikely sources of grace to others, especially if the solution to those wrongs is seen as getting even with one's enemies. As a young boy in the early 1950s I played a universal game fueled by racist-tinged World War II newsreels, documentaries, and Hollywood films that filled early television programming. When playing war, we would scream, "You dirty Japs, you killed my best friend," and then charge imagined enemies with imaginary machine guns blazing. This line, borrowed directly, I think, from a Hollywood B movie, never asked me to consider the truth about war or enemies. It bound me to a stereotype that called for revenge and death. Fortunately, it was a story I could stop living when my mother called me for dinner. Many others, including whole societies, have not been so lucky.

There is much about that central American success story that is not conducive to grace. In a society marked by win-or-lose competition, consumerism, self-absorption, and predatory economic practices, grace will often be seen as impractical and even weakness. The gospel of my rights, my needs, winner take all leaves little room for treating others better than they deserve. It diminishes our collective ability to live healthy lives. If we get only what we deserve from others, most of us will get less than we need. And we will give too little as well.

❃   ❃   ❃

Lastly, healthy life stories are hopeful stories. Every story worth living contains the possibility of a desirable outcome. If it is true that we are most drawn to stories of people in trouble, it is also true that our continuing interest depends on the possibility the person will survive that trouble, perhaps even triumph over it. Ultimately, both fatalism and cynicism are boring.

Hope is not mere wishing. It is a reasonable expectation based on past experience. We do not have to bury our heads in the sand to be hopeful; we need only draw reasonable conclusions from the outcome of other stories. If others have made it through circumstances similar to our own, then so might we. If others testify to finding a plot to their lives, then so might we. If others have found a meaningful end to their stories that validates the middle, then so might we. Discovering these aspects of others' stories depends, of course, on hearing them—which brings us back to the importance of community and sharing stories.

Though there is sometimes a tension between the requirement that a healthy life story be hopeful and that it also be truthful, there need be no contradiction. The basis for hope is not naive optimism, but a knowledge of other stories that give evidence that courage, perseverance, and faith are at least as strong as evil and misfortune, and often stronger. When things are bleakest in the Bible, for instance, they tell stories of God's faithfulness in the past, providing the reasonable hope of God's action on their behalf in the present and future. The hope resides not in wishing, but in history.

We do well to name those people who live a kind of life story we would like to emulate. They might range from heroic figures in history or literature to uncelebrated people from our own lives. An example for me of the former is Martin Luther King, Jr. We know enough about his private life to understand he was no saint, perhaps not even always faithful to his own stated values. But what a story he lived.

He was committed to truth in places where even a little accommodation to the lie would have made life much easier. His faith that truth transcended the momentary and the material freed him to act in ways that changed for the better everyday reality for millions of people. His amazing ability to extend grace to those who offered him hatred or indifference was rooted in his own sense of having been the recipient of divine grace, and this understanding provided a unique moral energy that distinguished him from other reformers of his day and ours.

And Martin Luther King's life story was nothing if not hopeful, able to portray the world exactly as it is and at the same time as it could be. This mixture of realism and hope is illustrated in the speech he made the night before he died. He admitted the possibility that he might be killed before the movement he led achieved its goals. At the same time, he said, "I've been to the mountaintop. . . . And I've seen the promised land" (*Dream* 203).

Such an example can encourage us to think more consciously about our own stories. We can follow Thoreau's advice to "live deliberately," to live the life we choose rather than the one that just happens. With him we can "front only the essential facts of life, and see if I could not learn what it had to teach, and not, when I came to die, discover that I had not lived" (135).

If something like King's life seems too remote or unattainable or dangerous—for heroes or models often pay a high price for their commitments—then we can look closer to home. What parent or friend or co-worker is living a life that can be instructive to your own? If one wishes to live a healthy life story, the choices lie before anyone with eyes to see and the will to act.

For we are both chosen by and choose our stories. In our earliest years, our stories choose us. Later we have the ability and freedom to choose our stories. Some, of course, cling to us more tightly than others.

We have no control over the stories into which we are born and little over those in which we are raised. They are as much an inheritance as our genetic code, creating roles for us to play as surely as our DNA maps a future for our bodies. The stories characteristic of a particular civilization, era, country, class, race, gender, religion, education, local community, and family welcome us, tell us who we are, and what we should do. In the beginning, our participation in these stories is as automatic and unconscious as our breathing. We in fact do not even perceive them as stories, but only as everyday, unexceptional experience, to be responded to as unthinkingly as the eye's pupil responds to the light.

The moment the young child becomes reflective, however, is the moment the child begins developing the ability to choose rather than simply inherit a story. At the heart of reflection is the weighing of multiple possibilities—possible explanations, possible choices, possible consequences. The first suspicion that something could be different than it is signals the initial stirrings of character and the potential to choose one's story.

The more we come to exercise our human powers, the more we are able to choose the stories in which we will continue to participate. Even young children have a limited but genuine ability to say yes or no to the stories around them. My father told me once, and only once, the story of what he said was the most shameful thing he ever did. He was one of a group of children surrounding and harassing a young girl. In the heat of the moment he spit on her, and was immediately sorry. The memory of it brings shame and sorrow to this day. That he spit on her was likely the reflexive participation in the collective cruelty of which groups are capable. That he felt shame was in part the realization that he could have acted differently.

That ability to act differently is the key to character and to healing or changing broken stories. We can change our stories only by changing our choices, which we are able to do only if we are real characters, and not merely automatons or victims. Freedom and responsibility are self-fulfilling understandings of the self. If we live as though we are free and responsible, then those become the qualities of our life. Even people who argue eloquently that humans are not free live their own lives as if they were. They make plans and choices, contemplate alternatives, express frustration and anger when events do not conform to their desires.

It is a responsible exercise of that freedom to act so as to heal a broken story or to replace it with a healthier one. Many of those who collectively spend billions of dollars chasing after evanescent echoes in their inner life of some shadowy *self* would do better to consider the stories in which they presently are characters and to choose those stories and actions that are most genuinely true, freeing, gracious, and hopeful. Such stories will more often put you in contact with others than with your elusive self. But an indirect consequence of such stories is that often you know yourself and your place for the first time.

7

All Stories Are Not Created Equal: Stories, Relativism, and Responsibility

[The modern world] has no story and so cannot entertain promises.
                                        Robert Jensen

We should publicly confess our attachment to certain names . . .
                                        Czeslaw Milosz

The contemporary world is in many ways hostile to healthy stories. In a relativistic climate we have a reduced ability to believe and act in any story except our own. And our own often seem to us fragmented and plotless. Unsure about our own story and skeptical of the relevance of others' stories, we live diminished and anxious lives. The best solution to this situation is to embrace the power of story to transcend differences by uniting us in shared experience that calls us to shared action. Healthy stories defeat isolation and nihilism by linking us to others and by encouraging us to be characters engaged in life and not mere spectators.

Hamlet had nothing on us when he complained, "The time is out of joint." We hear from every corner that the world is a mess, and our own experience often confirms it. Things may have been as bad or worse in the past, but we had collectively more resources to deal with it. When we look around for causes of our deep-seated uneasiness we are unlikely to think of our stories precisely because they are largely invisible to us. We are too busy living our stories to think much about them. Yet the mythologist Joseph Campbell speculates that the decline of story and story-related activities is a leading cause of our discontent: "It is possible that the failure of mythology and ritual to function effectively in our civilization may account for the high incidence among us of the malaise that has led to the characterization of our time as 'The Age of Anxiety' " (92). Without active participation in healthy stories we grow sick and whiny.

One legacy of both Western culture's classical and religious heritages is the belief that "we inhabit a narratable world" (Jensen 19). That is, we traditionally have conceived of reality as explainable, and that explanation has primarily taken the form of a story with a plot in which we are the characters. That belief depends on a number of supporting beliefs: that reality is at least in part knowable; that there are meaningful connections between events; that actions have consequences; that humans do most things by choice, not by irresistible compulsion; that we are therefore responsible; and so on. Many of these notions on which story is based, however, have fallen into disrepute in the modern world.

One reason our time is hard on stories is that we have made disunity into a virtue. Not only do we have much less consensus about the fundamental nature of things than has been traditional in human societies; we have lost much of our belief even in the desirability of consensus. It is often associated with stifling conformity, authoritarianism, denial of diversity, or compromise of principle. To be in broad agreement with others is to sacrifice one's sacred individuality at the altar of the herd.

This kind of individualism can both promote stories and eviscerate them. It promotes them by validating the unique story of each person, whether approved by the group or not. It can weaken stories by encouraging the individual to believe it doesn't matter what anyone else thinks. It does matter what others think because, like it or not, they are part of my story. I simply cannot be fully human by myself.

Healthy individualism and community should be natural allies. Two common enemies of individualism _and_ community are socialist collectivism and capitalist consumerism, false egalitarianisms that treat everyone as identical, devalued units. Individualism and community, in contrast, make each other possible. A healthy community needs active individuals with a strong sense of self and of their own story, and a strong sense of self is learned from the stories provided by a healthy community.

But exaggerated individualism, one of relativism's stepchildren, not only encourages me to disregard the views and values of others, it also subtly suggests the irrelevance of stories other than my own. If no one can tell me what to do, no one can teach me what to do either. If I cannot be corrected by others, because we all have our own views and values, I cannot learn from them. The same tolerance that rightfully allows every person or group their own story can unwittingly trivialize everyone's story if it leads to all of us being isolated in our unique worlds.

A student of mine, for instance, once refused to try to understand what Toni Morrison might be saying in her novel _Beloved_ on the grounds that it would be presumptuous of a white male to suggest he understood something written by an African-American woman. In short, he said, "This book wasn't written for me." When we absolutize our differences, to the neglect of our more fundamental commonalities, we end up not with healthy tolerance, but with alienated fragmentation or indifference.

Nothing is more important for our individual and collective well-being than telling each other our stories. A wide variety of stories should not simply be tolerated but sought out and prized. This conviction is at the heart of a healthy multiculturalism that wishes to celebrate the lives and accomplishments of all people and to give everyone an equal opportunity to participate in the common story.

But there is a crucial difference between healthy diversity and killing fragmentation. The former is possible only when all are allowed, as Silone insisted, to tell their own story in their own words. The latter occurs when the uniqueness of each story is taken as proof that only certain people can understand or profit from it: those of the right gender, or race, or class, or any other category. All stories will of course mean more to some than to others, but we greatly underestimate the power of story and of the human imagination if we think we can designate such things in advance.

Another enemy of story, coexisting uneasily with affirmations of individualism in our society, is a kind of selectively invoked determinism. As part of our modern flight from the responsibility inherent in being true characters, we willingly trade in our freedom to be relieved of our responsibility. Many of the governing conceptions of the human situation in the last 150 years have a strong deterministic bent that says we are what we are because of forces over which we have no control and perhaps even little awareness. Marx says we are the product of our class, Darwin of a blind process of natural selection, Freud of our unconscious. Other ideologies would have us believe we are defined by our gender or genetics or race.

Each of these views arises from powerful experiential truths, but each becomes a debilitating distortion if its claims rob us of our human responsibility. Viktor Frankl argues that the collective neurosis of our age is nihilism, a radical skepticism about the possibility of true knowledge and of moral claims, and that it is enhanced rather than cured by therapies that deny or diminish human freedom (131–33). It may provide temporary relief to blame your unhappiness on your upbringing, or your spouse, or your unconscious mind, or society, or the phases of the moon, but blaming will not cure what ails you.

Ceaseless blaming gives away too much of our power. It takes the keys of our destiny out of our own hands and places them in the hands of forces that are either hostile or indifferent to us. It both ignores the degree to which we have contributed to whatever state we are in and puts us at the mercy of others to change that state. Rather than responsible characters acting to shape our lives, we are static victims, waiting for someone else to determine our future. But if we are not responsible we are not free, and if we are not free we cannot be characters in meaningful stories.

None of this is intended to disparage the human need and right to cry out when one has been wronged and to point out the one who has mistreated you. It is simply a plea to make the cry only the first step. I think the African-American writer Zora Neale Hurston, who had more reasons than most to complain, had it right when she declared, "I am not tragically colored." Declaring that "the world is to the strong," she announces somewhat ambiguously, "I do not weep at the world—I am too busy sharpening my oyster knife" (153). Hurston was not diminishing the wrongs done to African-Americans. She was simply declaring something about her mode of response.

Another common platitude about stories, the flip side of the belief that every story is unique, is the assertion that all stories are equally true and valuable. This is simply false. Many stories convey life, others death. The stories we choose to spend our lives with are a reflection of our values and, therefore, our character (Booth 177). A healthy understanding of story can protect us from the paralysis and moral indifference of uncritical relativism.

Relativism is the distinguishing moral fingerprint of our time. It suffuses our public and private conversations in the way rationalism may have done in the Enlightenment or faith in the Middle Ages— only to a greater extent. It is the air we breathe.

Essentially, relativism denies the possibility of any significant truth claim being more than personal opinion. All assertions about truth and falsehood, good and evil, desirable and undesirable are expressions of individual preference, not statements about how things are. The validity of "should" and "ought" and even "is" stops at the tip of your nose. Depending on how it is applied, such a view can result in the claim that all stories are true—because truth is whatever anyone thinks it is—or that no stories are true, because the word "true" is meaningless if there is no such thing as untrue.

From another angle, relativism can support the view that only my truth is relevant and that no one can say "no" to me. The latter is expressed in melodramatic earnestness by Ayn Rand: "Many words have been granted me, and some are wise, and some are false, but only three are holy; 'I will it!' . . . Whatever road I take, the guiding star is within me; the guiding star and the lodestone which point the way. They point in but one direction. They point to me" (quoted in Midgley 98). Such views, while rarely stated so baldly, lie behind a host of common responses to the urgent moral and social issues of our day.

We are all relativists to a degree, and should be. But we should also reject the kind of dogmatic relativism that suggests there is no such thing as truth and falsehood or good and evil in themselves, and vilifies anyone who suggests otherwise. This kind of relativism, to which many retreat when pressed to make a difficult moral judgment, ultimately leaves us defenseless and powerless. No practicing moral relativist can lift a hand, or even a voice, against violence, aggression, racism, sexism, or any other evil in the world. If right and wrong are mere opinion, not rooted somehow in the nature of things, then Hitler was merely strongly opinionated and violent racists simply exercise their rights to live out their own views. (And don't invoke the "as long as it doesn't hurt anyone else" rule, because that's only an opinion, too.)

This kind of relativism is repugnant and widely rejected in its blatant forms, but is seductive and pleasing when disguised as tolerance or openness. Everyone who believes in tolerance as an essential virtue in a pluralistic society, and I am one, should be able to explain clearly what he or she will *not* tolerate and why. Those who will tolerate everything are of no use in fighting intolerance or in building a more just and humane society.

144

Dogmatic relativism leads not to healthy tolerance but to passivity, paralysis, and nihilism. This tendency is exacerbated when combined with the modern penchant, discussed earlier, for a kind of deterministic fatalism. Voltaire savagely satirized in the eighteenth century a kind of head-in-the-sand Christianity that foolishly defended God and the status quo by asserting, "Whatever is is right." In *Candide* he followed his naive hero from tragedy to tragedy as Voltaire mocked a view that seemed so indifferent to human suffering.

Ironically, that view is the unintended corollary of positions taken by many secularists today. Any behavior that can be explained as caused by something outside the conscious will of the individual— be that cause social, or psychological, or physical—is taken as *natural* and therefore morally blameless, perhaps even laudable. As social and natural scientists attempt to push more and more human behavior into this *morally free* zone, we find, as I recently did, even wife beaters referred to as "suffering from the disease of wife abuse." How, pray tell, can I be responsible if my actions are the result of sickness? It is a question that assumes only one possible answer.

Such passivity is a result of a relativism that encourages us to be spectators rather than characters. If you have your values and I have mine, and there is no legitimate way of judging between them, how can either of us justify trying to change anything? I cannot criticize anything in the world, because that implies my values have some claim on other people. And we are not likely even to change ourselves: by what criterion—all criteria being little more than whim— would we choose one potential self over another? Again, no one sees himself or herself in such a description. But who of us has not at times retreated behind the "Who's to say?" shrug when confronted with a difficult moral assessment or choice?

The great danger of being spectators rather than characters is made clear in the life and works of Elie Wiesel. Wiesel tells us over and over again that the Holocaust was possible only because millions of individuals decided it was none of their business. His greatest contempt, in works like *The Town Beyond the Wall,* is not directed at the killers but at the watchers. His protagonist in that novel returns to his Eastern European town years after the war to confront a man who had watched impassively from a window while he and his family were rounded up with other Jews. The man refuses to accept any guilt or feelings of shame for his behavior: "No, I tell you. I had a shocked feeling that I was a spectator at some sort of game—a game I didn't understand: a game you had all begun playing, you on one side, the Germans and the police on the other. I had nothing to do with it" (157).

The protagonist's response is Wiesel's judgment on every person who insists on remaining neutral in a world that cries out for action: "You're a shameful coward! You haven't got the courage to do either good or evil! The role of spectator suited you to perfection. They killed? You had nothing to do with it. They looted the houses like vultures? You had nothing to do with it. Your conscience is clear. 'Not guilty, your honor!' You're a disgusting coward! You hedge: you want to be on the winning side no matter what!" (158).

One measure of the sickness of our shared stories today is the degree to which curiosity has been displaced by voyeurism. The two are closely related but crucially different. Curiosity *involves* one in the thing being explored; it invites us into a relationship, and is a key ingredient in story. Voyeurism, on the other hand, keeps us at a distance, detached, making objects both of ourselves and of the thing observed. This turning of humans into objects is the root evil of voyeurism—pornography and television talk shows being two of the more common forms in our society today.

The habit of being an objective spectator is an invitation to skepticism and even nihilism. All of us are, at times, detached observers, storytellers perhaps more often than most. Healthy skepticism can be a form of protection. But when detached spectating becomes habitual unwillingness to act, and skepticism becomes inability to risk commitment, we are diminished as human beings and as characters in meaningful stories.

Seeing ourselves as such characters enhances our sense of accountability. Characters choose and their choices have consequences. A story that denies its characters any responsibility for those choices and consequences reduces their significance and humanity. (Is this why Thomas Hardy's Tess strikes so many as duller and less interesting than, say, Emily Brontë's Catherine?) If I have a sense of participating in a story with roots in the past, and of creating that story in the present as it is extended into the future, I am more likely to act in the world, rather than watch it go by.

Healthy stories are antideterministic. They refuse the conviction that everything is already decided, that there is nothing to be done. They are also antirelativistic. While celebrating the pluralism of many voices, they deny the passivity and paralysis that flow from treating truth as mere opinion and individual values as inconsequential beyond the nose of the individual. All stories, without exception, insist that a certain view of the world is true, and all the ones worth living call us to act on that truth.

Stories can free us from the paralysis of incomplete knowledge. A standard excuse for inaction is lack of certainty. Passivity and paralysis are often dressed up as modesty. Extreme skepticism, claiming to know nothing, is seen as more honest and therefore more honorable than trying to "impose your values" on the world. Having prided ourselves on our (moral) superiority to moralistic societies of the past—Puritan and Victorian, for instance, both being condemning adjectives—we have removed most of the ground for making any assertions at all, moral or otherwise. Fearful of affirming that which we cannot absolutely prove, we lead cautious and less meaningful lives.

Stories, on the other hand, teach us that characters usually must act without complete or certain knowledge. Huck Finn abandons his torturous attempts to know for certain what he should do, and simply decides to help Jim. This is not an argument for abandoning moral reasoning, but for not allowing prolonged and permanently inconclusive reflection to be an excuse for moral paralysis.

Furthermore, stories and storytellers are notoriously opinionated.

They have a point of view, an ax to grind, a vision to impart, a bone to pick, a complaint to lodge, a charge to level (*"J'accuse!"*), an itch to scratch, a bee in the bonnet, a cry of pain to share. When I was a boy, I was fascinated by those mothers of my friends who were loud and opinionated and slightly excessive (and even smoked!). They laughed out loud and said what they thought and had opinions on everything. Something told me they were more alive and useful than June Cleaver or Harriet Nelson or any of the television moms. They were so, I now believe, because they were characters—in the best sense of the word. If their judgments were not always right, they at least were the stuff of engaged human beings.

Unqualified relativism, determinism, and fear of acting on partial knowledge together lead to passivity, paralysis, and cynicism. Together they encourage us to be spectators rather than characters, to analyze but not to act. They are therefore the enemies of story and of people creating meaningful lives through participating in stories.

In his novel *One Day in the Life of Ivan Denisovich,* Solzhenitsyn asks a very important question with implications far beyond the frozen prison camp in Siberia out of which the question arises: "How can you expect a man who's warm to understand a man who's cold?" (34). This is a specific expression of a larger question: Can anyone understand—and care about—anyone else? And caring, can they act to help? Those who have inhaled deeply the modern mist of relativism, determinism, and moral timidity have no logical grounds for any answer except "No."

Solzhenitsyn, the storyteller, argues otherwise. In his *Nobel Lecture,* as we have seen, he holds writers as accountable as any other citizen for the evils that go on in their society. In fact they are more accountable because they have more resources with which to combat evil. The average person can resolve not to participate in the lies on which all violence is based, Solzhenitsyn argues. But the writer can do more, because the writer can vanquish lies. By telling the truth—Solzhenitsyn is not embarrassed by the word—stories encourage us to live by the truth. His closing citation in the *Nobel*

Lecture of a Russian proverb is the optimistic and courageous assertion of story generally: "One word of truth outweighs the world"
(34). Solzhenitsyn knows better than most how complex and hidden
the truth can be, and how brazenly optimistic such an assertion is,
but declares nonetheless, "On such a seemingly fantastic violation
of the law of the conservation of mass and energy are based both my
own activities and my appeal to the writers of the whole world."

Stories tell us that some ways of living are better than others.
Relativism—which is powerless to make an ethical distinction between the Nazi story and that of its victims—is of no help in
determining which stories to embrace. In a pluralistic world we
should listen to many stories, but as individuals and as societies we
cannot be indifferent to which we choose to live by.

Cynicism and dogmatic skepticism are not defeated by argument,
only by lives lived. Meaning resides less in abstract arguments than
in action in the world. The specific meaning of each of our stories is
discovered in the living. Even hard-core facts, Frankl argues, "will
be significant only as far as they are part of the human experience"
(19–20). The question "What is the best chess move?" is meaningless in the abstract, he points out, answerable only in the context of
a particular game. Similarly, the big questions of life can only be
answered in the context of our individual stories. And without a
story, it is not possible for us to answer at all.

Those answers are not plain and fixed. They will change in shape
and impact as our stories develop. Bettelheim argues that children
extract from a fairy tale what they need at a particular time of
hearing and that sometimes children will literally hear—or at least
remember—the story differently from the way it is told in order to
have it better fit their need (151–52). We all are drawn to the stories
that we need—or feel we need. _Huck Finn_ is only one of many that
can be read at every stage of one's life, and mean something more
each time.

That the meaning of our stories and their answers to life's questions change over time does not indicate that those meanings and
answers are insubstantial, only that our understanding is always

partial. Many of the truths of our life stories become clear only in the living. It is no accident that most cultures have valued the wisdom of the elderly. That wisdom is largely the wisdom of story. It is truth sifted from story-shaped experience. Our ability to understand stories should grow with age. Young people often see less in the stories of literature simply because they bring less life experience to them. That we so disproportionately value youth over age is another indication of the illness of our society, and another obstacle to healthy stories.

Seeing our lives in terms of story makes plain to us our connectedness. The importance of this connectedness is now widely recognized, after a period in which the rhetoric of individualism and relativism has too exclusively held the stage. The challenge is not to choose between individualism and community, but to encourage the healthy interdependence of the two. We have stockpiled enough self-absorption and romantic individualism to last us through many a winter. For a while now, we need to nurture and feed on stories of community.

It is a mark not only of our romanticism but of our arrested development that we so persistently see *society* or the community as primarily an evil, restrictive force against which we must rebel to protect our individual integrity. We are perpetual adolescents, whining endlessly that society is arrayed against our quest for happiness. In fact the opposite is more nearly true. Community, for all its flaws, is the only context in which we can live by any other law than survival of the most successful predator.

Our root complaint about community is that it will force us to do what we do not wish to do. This is sometimes true. Communities do, in fact, organize around laws and expectations—written and unwritten. But it is exactly those laws and expectations, when they are healthy, that should help you *know* what it is you want to do and what is worth wanting to do. And they are expressed most powerfully in story.

In Robert Bolt's *A Man for All Seasons,* Thomas More's daughter and a friend try to convince him to arrest a man who is going to betray More. He refuses on the grounds that even though the man is a scoundrel, he is under the protection of the law until he breaks it. The exchange reveals More's deep understanding of the degree to which communal law, rightly exercised, is a protection rather than a hindrance:

> *Alice:* While you talk, he's gone!
> *More:* And go he should, if he was the Devil himself, until he broke the law!
> *Roper:* So now you'd give the Devil benefit of law!
> *More:* Yes. What would you do? Cut a great road through the law to get after the Devil?
> *Roper:* I'd cut down every law in England to do that!
> *More:* Oh? And when the last law was down, and the Devil turned round on you—where would you hide, Roper, the laws all being flat? . . . d'you really think you could stand upright in the winds that would blow then? Yes, I'd give the Devil benefit of law, for my own safety's sake. (37–38)

More's friend had an Ayn Rand type of confidence in his ability to discern and do the right thing without help from anyone else. Thomas More saw that without the protection of the community-endorsed law, his friend was merely lunch meat for the Devil.

We cannot separate our individual story from the story of the community even if we wanted to. After all, you are only one character even in your own story. It is as though Ahab thought he could hunt Moby Dick alone in a rowboat. Even America's obsessive individualism is simply a story about ourselves that we have agreed on together. Nothing is more an expression of the group than the insistence that one is different from the group. Count the advertisers who invite you to join millions of others in being unique and rebellious by using their product.

One consequence of an awareness of our connectedness should be a greater sense of responsibility for others. If you are part of my story, and I am part of yours, then I cannot be indifferent to what happens to you—even from the standpoint of mere self-interest. Herein lie both a benefit and a danger in the current emphasis on pluralism and the uniqueness of everyone's story. It can emphasize our connectedness in ways that help us value each other more, or it can exaggerate our separateness in ways that leave us feeling suspicious and threatened.

The logical consequence of exaggerating our inability to understand each other because of our uniqueness is not merely isolation into separated groups but the isolation of every individual. For which of us is not different from everyone else by some category or other, and what gap is there larger than that between two minds? Each of our experiences in life is unique enough to ensure our isolation if difference is an absolute barrier to understanding.

Story has traditionally been our best vehicle for overcoming our inherent separateness. When prehistoric hunters and gatherers congregated around the fire at night to recount the adventures of the day, the stories, told in turn, bonded them together and pushed back the night. What they shared together was more important than what divided them. Our stories today must do no less.

We will be defined, as individuals and as a society, by the stories we choose to live and by those we value enough to pass on to the next generation. This is perhaps our ultimate responsibility as characters acting freely. What stories will we tell our children and why? What stories will they choose to tell in turn?

The institutions of every human society exist primarily to preserve the views and values of that society. To be civilized, as that society defines it, is to internalize these values and live one's life accordingly. And, as I have argued repeatedly, those views and values are best captured in stories, including some that encourage us to question our stories.

One example of this universal phenomenon is found in the biblical story of the crossing of the people of Israel into the Promised Land. Most people in Western culture are at least vaguely familiar with the story of the first miraculous crossing at the Red Sea (Sea of

Reeds)—thanks, in part, to Cecil B. DeMille's special effects. A second story is less well-known but even more illustrative of the role of stories in passing on the values of a culture. When the wandering tribes come to the edge of Canaan, they find the Jordan River at flood stage and impossible to cross. God tells Joshua to have the priests carrying the Ark of the Covenant walk into the river with the Ark. As the priests step into the water, we are told, the flow is cut off and they stand on dry ground in the middle of the river while the whole nation passes by. The story continues as follows:

> When all the people had crossed the river, the LORD said to Joshua, "Choose twelve men, one from each tribe. Tell them to take twelve stones from where the priests are standing in the middle of the Jordan and carry them to the place where you camp tonight."
>
> So Joshua called together the twelve men, one from each tribe, and told them, "Go into the middle of the Jordan in front of the Ark of the LORD your God. Each of you pick up one stone on your shoulder—twelve stones in all, one for each of the twelve tribes. These stones will be a memorial for you. In the future, when your children ask, 'What is the meaning of these stones?' tell them, 'They remind us that the Jordan River stopped flowing when the Ark of the LORD's Covenant went across.' These stones will stand as a memorial for the people of Israel forever." (Joshua 4:1–7)

This is a passage about the importance of memory and of telling stories. It expresses the traditional Jewish understanding of covenant, God _acting_ in behalf of his people, and is one of many warnings in the Bible against memory lapses.

The storyteller here is trying to convince his audience that when they remember who they are, where they have come from, and who their God is, they prosper. When they quit telling the stories, they no longer know who they are and disaster ensues. This is why God tells Joshua to have each of the tribes of Israel contribute a rock to commemorate God's provision in leading them across the Jordan River. The rock monument in their midst will cause the children of the next generation to ask, "Why are those rocks there?" That question will prompt the story, and a new generation will understand the power of God.

We, too, must build rock monuments, primarily in story form, to the values our experience has taught us are most crucial. The reflex claim is that while this might be possible at the individual level, we could never have consensus about common values at the societal level. Stand up at a public school board meeting, for instance, and make a statement in favor of teaching our children values, and the echo of your voice will still be in the air when someone retorts, "Whose values?" That is a perfectly necessary question to ask when it is really a question. Too often it is actually a statement meant to end debate, the assumption being that everyone's values are too unique and even contradictory to make agreement possible.

Is this really the case? Are our stories really so radically different from each other that we have no common ground? I don't believe it. What ethnic group, culture, religion, political organization, gender, age group, or body type does not value courage, or honesty, or compassion, or integrity, or friendship, or perseverance, or cooperation, or loyalty, or dependability, or fairness, or any number of other core virtues. If some social scientist comes racing in to say, "Indeed, the people of lower Pango Pango value none of these things," then I say so much the worse for lower Pango Pango. I will not allow inescapable pluralism to render me morally mute. I will not only make choices but will campaign for many of them, because my stories tell me they are important for more than just me.

At the same time, I will listen attentively to the stories of others. I will find that many of my values can also be found in their stories. I will find values in stories that I had not heard that will make me rethink my own and either change them or see them in a different way. This is not relativism; it is learning from others as we mutually seek what is true and good and beautiful.

Epilogue

The old deeds are done, old evil and old good have been made into stories, as plows turn up the river bottom . . .

Eudora Welty

Eudora Welty has written of her disappointment as a child in discovering that books of stories were created by people, that they "were not natural wonders, coming up of themselves like grass" (5). It is an understandable mistake. Stories *are* as natural as grass, and more widespread. Many things could be removed from our lives and we would still be human; stories are not one of them.

Stories receive us at birth, accompany us through the stages of life, and prepare us for death. They provide the context in which we learn who we are and what we are to do. They give pattern to otherwise chaotic experience, making it memorable and meaningful.

We *are* what we remember, and what we do with those memories. Scott Momaday says, "If I were to remember other things, I should be someone else" (63). Among the things he remembers is being brought by his father to see his great-grandmother. She is blind, sitting in a dark room. His father talks to her in Kiowa about him, and she reaches out to make contact with this young boy who will carry on in the world that she is leaving: "She is seated on the side of her bed, and my father brings me to stand directly in front of her. She reaches out for me and I place my hands in hers. *Eh neh*

neh neh neh. She begins to weep very softly in a high, thin, hollow voice. Her hands are little and soft. . . . Her voice is so delicate, so surely expressive of her deep feelings. Long afterwards I think: That was a wonderful and beautiful thing that happened in my life. There, on that warm, distant afternoon: an old woman and a child, holding hands across the generations. There is great good in such a remembrance; I cannot imagine that it might have been lost upon me" (65).

Yes, there is great good in such a memory—for Momaday, for his community, and for us. Such remembrances are the raw material of story and they remind us of many things that are fatal to forget. They remind us that we are connected, that we are not alone, that someone cares enough to weep over us. They remind us that there are expectations for us, and that this is good. They remind us that life passes quickly and that, as characters, we must do what our stories call us to do, because soon *we* will be the old ones covering the young with our tears.

Such remembrances also remind us that healthy stories protect and nurture us. Another Native American writer, Diane Glancy, affirms in an unpublished prose poem how stories come to live with and take care of us: "So now the story has made camp in your heads. The story will hunt for you and at night its campfires will keep you alive."

In cultures where the sense of community is still strong, stories are prized as the vehicle for instruction in those things on which the life of the community depends. African-American scholar Henry Mitchell says, "All my life I have been blessed by parents, grandparents, and others who felt an obligation to equip the young with a certain wisdom about life" (xiii). That wisdom is captured in stories, and in tribal societies they are the guardian of the public, and therefore also the individual, good: "no child was considered equipped or even fit for life who was not steeped in this oral tradition" (8).

To the extent that we have lost our confidence that we possess "a certain wisdom about life," we abandon the young to shift for themselves in a relativistic world and we testify to the thinness of our own story. The good news is that it doesn't have to be this way. Stories celebrate our freedom to choose—to be characters—a wonderful, terrible freedom that makes it possible for things to be different.

In his _Nobel Lecture,_ Solzhenitsyn reflects on the role of stories, and art generally, in the modern world, and identifies four things literature can do to help heal a violent, fragmented, alienated world. First, it preserves memory, without which we forget who we are. In addition, it helps us to see ourselves accurately, diluting our human tendency to self-delusion. Further, it gives us a vehicle for overcoming our radical separateness and the relativism of values, offering something for common contemplation that shows us our potential for agreement and community. Lastly, as we have seen, art and stories can vanquish lies, including the lies that provide the needed cover for violence and oppression.

We have claimed all this for story and more. Elie Wiesel writes to preserve the memory of those who died before he had a chance to say goodbye, and to remind us of what was done to them so that it will never be done again. Toni Morrison helps us see ourselves accurately and our history of oppression without illusion. Martin Luther King told the nation a story about itself that allowed a great variety of people to aspire to the common virtues of justice and freedom. Through Huck Finn and Jim, Mark Twain exposed a central lie of his time, one that has not completely been defeated.

These are some of our national storytellers. Their stories are added to the ones I have heard since birth—from my father and mother; from Uncle Remus and the Brothers Grimm; from my first teachers and preachers; from my friends and kindred spirits; stories from those long dead and from those whose lives were cut short; stories from the dark side and stories from the light. All are part of my story now, and together they make it possible for me to see a plot to my life and to have the boldness to declare myself a character— with all the meaning and responsibility that entails.

Scott Momaday was taken to Devils Tower as an infant. He was named after the boy in the story who chased his sisters into the sky. Now, wherever he is, Momaday can look at their constellation in the heavens and see kindred and know he is at home. If you and I root ourselves in healthy stories, we can know the same.

Appendix
Identifying Your Defining Stories

This is not a self-help book, but it does have the potential to be helpful. By identifying the stories that form us we can better understand ourselves and others, can more purposefully live the stories that sustain us, and can heal or replace the stories that do us harm. Knowing our stories more fully makes us better able to be active characters in those stories rather than passive spectators.

The questions below are story prompts. Give each one enough time to allow the stories to arise. Some will have been long forgotten, others will be seen as stories for the first time. Evaluate each one for its life- and character-shaping effects: what lessons or morals are taught, what values are implied, what is being celebrated or warned against, what view of the world comes through, what effect has it had on you, how has it shaped you as a character?

Because each of our lives is unique, you may have to adapt these questions to fit your own circumstances.

I. FAMILY STORIES

A family knows itself to be a family through its shared stories. When we speak of being related, we are speaking of the relationship of characters in interwoven stories. Our understanding of who we are begins with the stories the family tells to us and tells about us.

The following questions are prompts for identifying important family stories (including the extended family) and other stories of childhood. (The tense of the question might vary depending on your age.)

1. What stories are (were) told most often in your family? Why do you think these are told more often than others? What do they reveal about your family?

2. What are some of the earliest stories you remember being told in the family?

3. Do your family stories establish heroes, villains, rogues, martyrs, or some other type? Are you any of these in the stories?

4. What stories are told about you in the family? How do they depict you? How do you feel when you hear them? What significance do you think they have?

5. How was the concept *good person* defined in your home? Bad person? What stories were told to illustrate?

6. How did the stories of your family depict the world outside your family (e.g., a hostile or dangerous place, a place of opportunity, etc.)?

7. What were your recurring fantasies as a child? Any relation to your present fantasies?

8. What stories do you know about your father and mother before they were married? Before they had children? Do they provide any clues to *your* character?

9. Has your attitude toward any of the family stories changed over the years?

10. What are your *favorite* family stories?

11. What are your favorite stories about yourself as a child? Which do you dislike the most? Why? Which do you yourself tell?

12. Are there family photographs which capture part of the story of your family or childhood?

13. Which family stories do you think helped shape who you are today—how you see the world, how you see yourself, what your values are, how you relate to others?

14. Which family stories do you embrace and celebrate? Which do you now see as unhealthy and distorted?

15. What stories are suppressed in your family? Why are they not told?

16. What qualities would you like to see in your family stories in the future? What choices of yours will make it more likely?

17. The first step outside the family is into the neighborhood. Explore the above questions in terms of neighbors, friends, and peers. What _adventure stories_ from childhood and adolescence stand out?

II. SCHOOL STORIES

Education is primarily storytelling. Every culture prizes certain stories above others and puts those stories at the center of that long process of creating citizens that we call education. Great changes in a society are always accompanied by great changes in the stories we tell, or no longer tell, in school. Our individual lives and conceptions are significantly shaped by the stories we hear and embrace in the classroom.

1. What is the earliest story you remember hearing in school?

2. What stories made a strong, immediate impression, perhaps changing the way you thought or felt?

3. Which of your teachers were the best storytellers? What kind of stories did they tell? What specific stories do you remember? What impact did these teachers have on you?

4. Who were some of the heroes and villains of school stories? Do you still see them this way?

5. What values or outlooks do you presently hold that you think were influenced by the stories you heard in school? Can you link any of them to specific stories?

6. Can you think of school stories which influenced your behavior? Your view of yourself or your possibilities in life? Your values?

7. What stories did you _not_ hear in school that you now believe you should have heard?

8. What stories did you hear that are no longer being told? Which should be and which should not?

9. Describe your early experiences in reading on your own?

10. What kinds of things did you read on your own during the school years? Do you now see any significance to the stories you chose on your own as compared with the stories you were assigned for school?

11. If you had a chance now to read one story to young children in school, which would it be? To adolescents? To young adults? Why?

12. In addition to stories you hear or read in school, the school experience itself generates many stories. What are some of the stories from your life *at* school which you now think of as important?

13. Which schoolmates or teachers were important characters in your school years? What influence did they have on you, for good or bad? Can you think of specific stories that illustrate that influence?

14. Is there a discernible plot or theme to your school experience over the years?

15. Did you try to imitate in your own life any of the stories you learned at school?

16. What specific school experiences can you identify that helped shape your character in some way?

III. RELIGIOUS STORIES

The great majority of people in the world have grown up with some degree of religious influence. The church, the synagogue, the mosque, the shrine, and the temple tell the most powerful stories of all: stories of first things and last things, of transcendent and eternal things, of innermost and secret things, of things mysterious and things profound. They also tell us what to do when our pet frog dies.

Adapt these questions to your particular religious experience.

1. What are the earliest stories from church that you remember?

2. What was your childhood response to stories of the miraculous and supernatural?

3. What were your favorite stories from the Bible (or other sacred scripture) at various times in your life? Why do you think you liked these best?

4. What were your favorite characters from the Bible? Why were they favorites? Did you identify with them? Find them very different from you? What acts did they perform or values did they embody that attracted you?

5. How has your attitude toward these stories and characters changed over time?

6. What was your early image of God? What stories—from the Bible, church, or family—contributed to that image?

7. What is your present image of God? What stories—from any source—have contributed to the change?

8. What stories of your religious upbringing do you still value? Why these? How are they currently evident in your life? How could they be more so?

9. What stories of personal religious experience were told in your family? To what effect in your own life?

10. What are some of your own stories of religious experience? How have these experiences and stories shaped your life? What is your present attitude toward them?

11. As with school, your own experience in church and at home creates stories. Look at questions 12–16 under the school section and ask the same about church or about the religious experience in the home.

IV. STORIES OF THE ZEITGEIST AND POPULAR CULTURE

People we don't even know surround us with their stories. They flow from the television, radio, video recorder, movies—even from the Internet. They insinuate themselves into our lives through books, magazines, journals, manifestos, and street-corner tracts. They come to us as films, dramas, documentaries, songs, advertisements, and news. All of them advocate something: an attitude, an outlook, a value, a fact, a product, an experience. We do well to ask ourselves what these stories are doing to us.

1. What are your favorite novels or short stories; your favorite myths, folktales, and children's stories? Why do you like them? Have any of them changed, even slightly, the way you think about yourself or life? What characters have you closely identified with and why? (Ask the same questions about poetry, drama, film, and other art forms.)

2. Can you identify any television shows, single or a series, that have had an impact on you? What was powerful about them? Who were the memorable characters? How did they affect you and why?

3. How would you characterize the kind and quality of stories being told in popular culture and the media? What values recur in these stories? Has this changed in your lifetime? How do you account for the change?

4. What kind of stories in the popular media are you drawn to? What kind disturb you? What might this reveal about you?

5. What stories do advertisers tell us? About America? About our bodies? About our values? About what we want and what we need? About what constitutes success or happiness? Can you identify any attitude or outlook you hold, perhaps unconsciously up to now, that has been influenced by stories from advertising?

6. How have your political, economic, and social views been influenced by stories? What relevant stories did you hear growing up; what stories from popular culture and the media? What stories do you now tell to support your views? What stories from your own life experience are relevant here? Who are your heroes in these areas? What choices did they make that you admire? Who are your villains?

V. LIFE-DEFINING STORIES

Though many stories contribute to who we are, a few large-scale, overarching life narratives often control the way we see the world and ourselves in it. If these are essentially healthy, our lives have great potential for meaning and satisfaction. If not, we are likely to be perpetually dissatisfied. Identifying these life-defining stories can be a first step either to affirming or to changing them.

1. Can you identify some of the large-scale, defining stories in your life? (Think of some of the preceding categories: family, education, religion, politics, popular culture, and so on.)

2. What qualities do you want the story of your life to have? What qualities does it currently have?

3. Is your present story truthful, freeing, gracious, and hopeful, as explored in Chapter 6?

4. Do you detect a plot to your life? Describe it. What are some of the key events (large or small)?

5. Is the plot of your life to this point one that makes likely the future you desire?

6. How would you like your story to end? What would you like to be said of your life by those who live after you? What can you do to make that more likely?

7. How would you describe yourself as a character in your own story? What choices have you made in the past that have contributed to your story being what it now is? What choices can you make to have it be what you want it to be in the future?

8. Who are other important characters in your story? What role do they play? Have they enhanced or diminished your story?

9. In whose story have you been an important character? Have you enhanced or diminished their story? What actions can you take to make their story even better?

10. Who else knows your story?

11. What healthy and healing stories are available to you that you might want to make part of your own?

Notes

CHAPTER 2

1. This impulse to explain is the impetus for most stories, as is particularly clear in those special kinds of stories focusing on origins which we call myth.

2. For an extended discussion of the limits of the reasoning process, especially as it relates to religious faith, see my *The Myth of Certainty,* Zondervan. Better yet, read Kierkegaard.

3. Actually, MacIntyre and other philosophers argue that rationality itself is a culturally shaped approach to life that is dependent on a long history of stories.

4. Ideas can be *experienced.* The pure realization and entertainment of an abstract idea can be as much an experience as is a physical event, but in most cases powerful ideas are incarnated in some form of story. Philosophy and abstract reasoning often revert to story to substantiate their theories.

CHAPTER 3

1. Wayne Booth's *The Company We Keep* is a great resource for those interested in story's character-forming potential and its relation to ethics.

2. Booth says he frequently asks audiences to name the novels that have caused them to want to change their character or their conduct (278) and that he always gets eager responses, with only an occasional protest from an academic that novels cannot change anyone.

3. Science generally and psychology in particular have been forced to recognize the impossibility of this quest for objectivity. No human activity is objective or value-free. Even supposedly neutral descriptions of personality hide unstated values. Assertiveness, for instance, is much more likely to be seen as healthy and desirable for a United States psychologist than for a Japanese one.

4. It is not only psychology which has attempted (unsuccessfully) to remove value judgments in order to be more objective. Academic literary study joined the flight from values under pressure from science and uncritical relativism. The central characters in stories could no longer be called heroes, but only protago-

nists. One can only expect a character to struggle. To want more is seen as naive, old-fashioned, maybe even reactionary.

This symbolic shift in terminology from hero to protagonist—and many more significant developments in the humanities generally—parallels the shift in psychology from character to personality. It is not simply a reflection of the tendency of modern writers to create decidedly unheroic characters; it is symptomatic of the common nervousness among intellectuals about the place of values—personal and public—in academic discourse. This trend has been reversed somewhat with the rise of literature and intellectual criticism from people of color and feminists.

5. Which is not to say that codes and rational abstractions have no use. We need both stories and codes. Codes and rational abstractions can helpfully clarify and epitomize story, but they have little power or significance when cut off from the stories out of which they arise. Even the Ten Commandments depend for their cogency and authority on the story of the Israelites' exodus from Egypt in which they are embedded. Emphasizing story doesn't exclude rational analysis. *Part* of the attraction of a story can be its appeal to reason (but only part). Reason can even have a sort of veto power over the process, but it does not dominate it; nor is it the primary faculty to which the appeal is directed.

CHAPTER 4

1. Consider Oskar Schindler in *Schindler's List*. People *call* him a good man and it begins to change the way he thinks of himself and of the possibilities for his life. His early, tentative acts of goodness (often done for selfish reasons) initiate a direction in his life that prepares the ground for subsequent and more conscious acts of courage and compassion.

2. There are a number of words for time in the New Testament, and kairos is not always used only in the special way described here. Despite such variation, the basic distinction I am making here is commonly accepted.

CHAPTER 5

1. Throughout the twentieth century an increasing number of stories have very pointedly kept us at an emotional distance from their characters. These stories are an expression, I believe, of our diminished confidence in the human experiment. They are legitimate stories, but they will never be the ones we value most.

Works Cited

CHAPTER 1

Crites, Stephen. "The Narrative Quality of Experience." *Journal of the American Academy of Religion* 39 (1971): 291–311.

Forster, E. M. *Aspects of the Novel.* New York: Harcourt, 1955.

MacIntyre, Alasdair. *After Virtue.* 1981. Notre Dame, Ind.: U of Notre Dame P, 1984.

Ríos, Albert. *Modern Poems.* Eds. Richard Ellmann and Robert O'Clair. 1973. New York: Norton, 1989.

Twain, Mark. "How to Tell a Story." *Norton Anthology of American Literature* (shorter). Eds. Nina Baym, et al. 1979. New York: Norton, 1989.

CHAPTER 2

Crites, Stephen. "The Narrative Quality of Experience." *Journal of the American Academy of Religion* 39 (1971): 291–311.

Griffin, Susan. *Made from This Earth: An Anthology of Writings.* New York: Harper, 1982.

Hauerwas, Stanley, and David Burrell. *Truthfulness and Tragedy: Further Investigations in Christian Ethics.* Notre Dame, Ind.: U of Notre Dame P, 1977.

Lawrence, D. H. "Why the Novel Matters." *Selected Literary Criticism.* Ed. Anthony Beal. New York: Viking, 1966.

Metz, Johann Baptist. "A Short Apology of Narrative." *Concilium* 85 (1973): 84–96.

Momaday, N. Scott. *House Made of Dawn.* New York: Harper, 1968.

———. *The Names: A Memoir.* New York: Harper, 1976.

Nussbaum, Martha. "Narrative Emotions: Beckett's Genealogy of Love." *Ethics* 98 (1988): 225–54.

Price, Reynolds. *A Palpable God: Thirty Stories Translated from the Bible. With an Essay on the Origins and Life of Narrative.* New York: Atheneum, 1978.

169

Wiesel, Eli. *Legends of Our Time.* New York: Avon, 1968.

Woiwode, Larry. "Acceptance Speech: The Theodore Roosevelt Rough Rider Award." *The Bias Report* 4.10 (1992): 3–6.

CHAPTER 3

Allport, Gordon. *Personality: A Psychological Interpretation.* New York: Holt, 1937.

———. *Pattern and Growth in Personality.* New York: Holt, 1961.

Bettelheim, Bruno. *The Uses of Enchantment: The Meaning and Importance of Fairy Tales.* 1976. New York: Random, 1989.

Booth, Wayne. *The Company We Keep: An Ethics of Fiction.* Berkeley: U of California P, 1988.

Coles, Robert. *The Call of Stories: Teaching and the Moral Imagination.* Boston: Houghton, 1989.

Hauerwas, Stanley, and David Burrell. *Truthfulness and Tragedy: Further Investigations in Christian Ethics.* Notre Dame, Ind.: U of Notre Dame, 1977.

Price, Reynolds. *A Palpable God: Thirty Stories Translated from the Bible. With an Essay on the Origins and Life of Narrative.* New York: Atheneum, 1978.

Taylor, Daniel. *Letters to My Children: A Father Passes on His Values.* Downers Grove, Ill.: InterVarsity P, 1989.

Twain, Mark [Samuel Langhorne Clemens]. *Adventures of Huckleberry Finn.* Ed. Sculley Bradley. 1962. New York: Norton, 1977.

CHAPTER 4

Barth, John. *Lost in the Funhouse: Fiction for Print, Tape, Live Voice.* New York: Doubleday, 1968.

Boles, Darcy. *Storycrafting.* Cincinnati: Writer's Digest, 1984.

Camus, Albert. *The Myth of Sisyphus and Other Essays.* Trans. Justin O'Brien. New York: Vintage, 1955.

Eliot, T. S. "Burnt Norton." *The Complete Poems and Plays 1909–1950.* New York: Harcourt, 1962.

———. *Murder in the Cathedral.* Ibid.

Frye, Northrup. "The Archetypes of Literature." Ed. David H. Richter. *The Critical Tradition: Classic Texts and Contemporary Trends.* New York: St. Martin's, 1989. 677–85.

James, Henry. "The Art of Fiction." *The Art of Fiction and Other Essays.* Ed. Morris Roberts. New York: Oxford UP, 1948.

Kermode, Frank. *The Sense of an Ending: Studies in the Theory of Fiction.* New York: Oxford UP, 1967.

King, Martin Luther, Jr. *Martin Luther King: An Amazing Grace.* Videocassette. Prod. Gil Noble. ABC. WABC, New York. n.d. 58 min.

Kittel, Gerhard. *Theological Dictionary of the New Testament.* Vol. 3. Grand Rapids, Mich.: Eerdmans, 1965. 10 vols. See also *The New International Dic-*

tionary of New Testament Theology. Ed. Colin Brown. Vol. 3. Grand Rapids, Mich.: Zondervan, 1986. 4 vols. 833–39.

MacIntyre, Alasdair. _After Virtue._ 1981. Notre Dame, Ind.: U of Notre Dame P, 1984.

McAdams, Dan P. _Stories We Live By: Personal Myths and the Making of the Self._ New York: Morrow, 1993.

Price, Reynolds. _A Palpable God: Thirty Stories Translated from the Bible. With an Essay on the Origins and Life of Narrative._ New York: Atheneum, 1978.

Rouse, John. _The Completed Gesture: Myth, Character, and Education._ New York: Skyline, 1978.

Twain, Mark [Samuel Langhorne Clemens]. _Adventures of Huckleberry Finn._ Ed. Sculley Bradley. 1962. New York: Norton, 1977.

CHAPTER 5

Augustine. _Confessions._ Trans. R. S. Pine-Coffin. Harmondsworth: Penguin, 1966.

Eliot, T. S. "Tradition and the Individual Talent." _Selected Essays._ New York: Harcourt, 1960.

Hauerwas, Stanley, and David Burrell. _Truthfulness and Tragedy: Further Investigations in Christian Ethics._ Notre Dame, Ind.: U of Notre Dame P, 1977.

McAdams, Dan P. _Stories We Live By: Personal Myths and the Making of the Self._ New York: Morrow, 1993.

Root, Michael. "The Narrative Structure of Soteriology." _Modern Theology_ 2 (1986): 145–57.

Stone, Elizabeth. _Black Sheep and Kissing Cousins: How Our Family Stories Shape Us._ New York: Penguin, 1988.

Wiesel, Elie. _Night._ 1960. New York: Avon, 1969.

CHAPTER 6

Barth, Karl. "The Gift of Freedom: Foundation of Evangelical Ethics." _The Humanity of God._ Trans. Thomas Weiser. Richmond, Va.: John Knox, 1964.

Berry, Wendell. _Sex, Economy, Freedom, and Community._ New York: Pantheon, 1993.

Bettelheim, Bruno. _The Uses of Enchantment: The Meaning and Importance of Fairy Tales._ 1976. New York: Random, 1989.

Carver, Raymond. _Where I'm Calling From: New and Selected Stories._ New York: Random, 1989.

Conrad, Joseph. Preface. _The Nigger of the Narcissus._ New York: Collier, 1962.

Crites, Stephen. "The Narrative Quality of Experience." _Journal of the American Academy of Religion_ 39 (1971): 291–311.

Hurston, Zora Neale. _Their Eyes Were Watching God._ 1937. New York: Harper, 1990.

King, Martin Luther, Jr. *Martin Luther King: An Amazing Grace.* Videocassette. Prod. Gil Noble. ABC. WABC, New York. n.d. 58 min.

———. *I Have a Dream: Writings and Speeches That Changed the World.* Ed. James Melvin Washington. Glenview, Ill.: Scott, Foresman, 1992.

MacIntyre, Alasdair. *After Virtue.* 1981. Notre Dame, Ind.: U of Notre Dame P, 1984.

Marty, Martin E. *By Way of Response.* Nashville: Abingdon, 1981.

Momaday, N. Scott. *The Names: A Memoir.* New York: Harper, 1976.

Moyers, Bill. "The Living Language." *Moyers: The Power of the Word.* Dir. Robert A. Miller. New Jersey Network and WNET, New York. 22 Sept. 1989.

Rich, Adrienne. "Blood, Bread, and Poetry: The Location of the Poet." *Adrienne Rich's Poetry and Prose.* Ed. Barbara Charlesworth Gelphi and Albert Gelphi. New York: Norton, 1993. 239–52.

Silko, Leslie Marmon. *Ceremony.* New York: Penguin, 1977.

Silone, Ignazio. Foreword. *Fontamara.* Trans. Eric Mosbacher. New York: NAL, 1981.

Thoreau, Henry David. *Walden and Civil Disobedience.* New York: Penguin, 1983.

Troupe, Quincy. *Weather Reports: New and Selected Poems by Quincy Troupe.* New York: Harlem River P, 1991.

Wiesel, Elie. *The Gates of the Forest.* Trans. Frances Frenaye. New York: Holt, 1966.

Wordsworth, William. *Wordsworth: Poetical Works.* Eds. Thomas Hutchinson, and Ernest Selincourt. New York: Oxford UP, 1969.

CHAPTER 7

Bettelheim, Bruno. *The Uses of Enchantment: The Meaning and Importance of Fairy Tales.* 1976. New York: Random, 1989.

Bolt, Robert. *A Man for All Seasons.* New York: Vintage, 1962.

Booth, Wayne. *The Company We Keep: An Ethics of Fiction.* Berkeley: U of California P, 1988.

Campbell, Joseph. *The Mask of God: Primitive Mythology.* 1959. New York: Penguin, 1976.

Frankl, Viktor. *Man's Search for Meaning: An Introduction to Logotherapy.* Trans. Ilse Lasch. 1959. New York: Simon and Schuster, 1984.

Hurston, Zora Neale. "How It Feels to Be Colored Me." *I Love Myself When I Am Laughing.* Ed. Alice Walker. New York: Feminist, 1979.

Jensen, Robert W. "How the World Lost Its Story." *First Things* 36 (1993): 19–24.

Midgley, Mary. *Can't We Make Moral Judgements?* New York: St. Martin's, 1993.

Solzhenitsyn, Alexander. *Nobel Lecture.* Trans. F. D. Reeve. New York: Farrar, 1972.

———. *One Day in the Life of Ivan Denisovich.* Trans. Ralph Parker. New York: NAL, 1963.

Wiesel, Elie. *The Town Beyond the Wall.* Trans. Stephen Becker. New York: Holt, 1964.

EPILOGUE

Mitchell, Henry H., and Nicholas C. Cooper-Lewter. *Soul Theology: The Heart of American Black Culture.* San Francisco: Harper, 1986.

Momaday, N. Scott. *The Names: A Memoir.* New York: Harper, 1976.

Solzhenitsyn, Alexander. *Nobel Lecture.* Trans. F. D. Reeve. New York: Farrar, 1972.

Welty, Eudora. *One Writer's Beginnings.* Cambridge: Harvard UP, 1984.

Index

Actions. *See* Significant actions
Adam (first man), 3
Adorno, Theodor, 39
Adventures of Huckleberry Finn
  (Twain), 43–45, 47, 48, 85, 149
Adventure stories, 161
Ahab (fictional character), 42, 72, 151
Allport, Gordon, 51–52
Ambrose (bishop of Milan), 87
American history, 12
American success story, 129–30, 134
Aristotle, 60, 73
Arnold, Matthew, 103
Assertiveness, value of, 167
Audiences. *See* Listening, value of
Augustine, Jane, 113
Augustine, St., 57, 86–87, 101, 111,
  126
Auschwitz, 18, 94, 98–99

Baal Shem-Tov, Rabbi Israel, 113,
  115
Baldwin, James, 126, 127
Bambi (fictional character), 34
Barth, John, 74
Barth, Karl, 108, 131
Beauvoir, Simone de, 126
Becket, Thomas à, 76
Beginnings, of stories, 60–62, 69, 73
Belief
  importance of, 77–78
  in stories, 16–17, 29, 116

Beloved (Morrison), 141
Beowulf (fictional character), 20
Berlin Wall, fall of, 14
Berry, Wendell, 131
Bettelheim, Bruno, 46, 128, 149
Big Bad Wolf (fictional character), 9,
  91
Billy Budd (Melville), 19
Blaming, negative impact of, 142–43
Bolt, Robert, 150
Booth, Wayne, 42, 143, 167
Bread and Wine (Silone), 119
Broken stories, healing, 3, 84–85,
  113–38
Brontë, Emily, 147
Brown, John, 101, 102, 111
Buber, Martin, 115, 116, 120
Burrell, David, 33, 54, 88

Campbell, Joseph, 140
Camus, Albert, 74, 96, 97, 111
Candide (Voltaire), 145
Carver, Raymond, 132
Cassandra (legendary character), 42
Catherine (fictional character), 147
Caulfield, Holden (fictional
  character), 47
Celie (fictional character), 131
Ceremony (Silko), 123–24
Change, 17–20
  and character, 42
Character(s), 15, 41–56

and beginnings, 61
and change, 42
choices of, 2, 42–43, 46, 53–55,
    63, 67, 69, 70, 125, 128, 147,
    157
defined, 18–19
emotional distance from, 168
heroes vs. protagonists, 167–68
and incident, 64
and middle, 63
and morality, 44–48
vs. personality, 2, 41, 51–53, 56,
    125, 168
in popular culture, 51–53, 56
in shared public stories, 81
vs. spectators, 3–4, 145–46
and suffering, 49–50
Choice(s)
of characters, 2, 42–43, 46, 53–55,
    63, 67, 69, 70, 125, 128, 147,
    157
consequences of, 63, 67, 90–92,
    147
Christ. *See* Jesus Christ
Christianity, 67, 86–87, 102–4, 122,
    145
Churchill, Winston, 8
Cinderella (fictional character), 9
Circumstances, important, 17
Claggart (fictional character), 19
Cleaver, June, 148
Codes, function of, 53, 168
Coles, Robert, 47, 85
Colliding stories, 13–14
Color Purple, The (Walker), 100, 131
Commitment, importance of, 77–78
Community
    bonding in, 122
    and individualism, 150–51
    and self, 141
Community stories, healing power in,
    114–19, 125, 156
Company We Keep, The (Booth), 167
Confessions (Augustine), 86
Conflicts, in middle, 63
Connectedness, importance of, 21,
    60, 85, 122, 150–52

Connor, Bull, 71
Conrad, Joseph, 129
Conroy, Gabriel, 109
Consensus, desirability of, 140
Consequences, of choices, 63, 67,
    90–92, 147
Core stories, 125
Crites, Stephen, 20, 27, 126
Crockett, Davy, 79–80
Cultures, 82
    ravaged, 122–24
    See also Popular culture
Curiosity, vs. voyeurism, 146

Dante, 105
Darwin, Charles, 64, 142
David (king of Hebrews), 132
"Dead, The" (Conroy), 109
"Declaration of Independence," 129
Defining stories. *See* Life-defining
    stories
Dehumanization, 117–19
DeMille, Cecil B., 153
Descartes, René, 25, 98
Determinism, 142, 145
Dickens, Charles, 96
Dick and Jane (fictional characters),
    12
Dinesen, Isak, 5
Disconnectedness, 74–75
Disjunction, 73–75
Disney, Walt, 90, 91
Diversity, vs. fragmentation, 141–42
Dodgers (baseball team), 89, 92, 93
Douglas, Widow (fictional character),
    63
Dream. See I Have a Dream
Drysdale, Don, 111

Ecclesiastes, 75
Edna (fictional character), 19
Education. *See* School stories
Edwards, Michael, 79
Einstein, Albert, 16
Eisenhower, Dwight, 62
Eliot, T. S., 68, 87
Emotions, importance of, 33–34, 130

Empathy
  and grace, 133–34
  in listening, 120
Ending, of stories, 69–73, 74, 135
  See also Imagined ends, of story
Endon, Mr. (fictional character), 18
Enlightenment, 143
Environmentalists, 34–35
Ericson, Edward, 104
Ethical injunctions, 54
Ethical knowledge, 30–31
Evans, Dr. Arthur, 104–11
Evil. _See_ Good and evil
Experience, 85
  of ideas, 167
  and knowledge, 26–27, 33
  power of, 120–21
  shared, 64–65
Explanations, in stories, 85

Facts, vs. stories, 80–83
Failed stories. _See_ Broken stories,
  healing
Fairy tales, 90–91, 128, 149
Faith, importance of, 77–78
  See also Religious stories
Family stories, 8–11, 101–2, 159–61
Fatalism. _See_ Determinism
Faulkner, William, 96
Faustus (legendary character), 20
Fiction, vs. reality, 20
Finn, Huckleberry (fictional
  character), 43–45, 47, 54, 55,
  63–66, 73, 85, 111, 147, 157
Fontamara (Silone), 119–20
Forster, E. M., 17
Four Quartets (Eliot), 68
Fragmentation, vs. diversity, 141–42
Frankl, Victor, 142, 149
Freedom, 2, 64
  vs. responsibility, 142–43
  and self, 137–38
  and significant actions, 130–32
Freud, Sigmund, 52, 61, 64, 142
Frost, Robert, 16, 120
Frye, Northrup, 58

Gardner, John, 57
Gates to the Forest, The (Wiesel),
  113–14
Gestalt psychology, 20
Glancy, Diane, 156
Good and evil, 19, 31–32, 48, 90,
  96–98
Good stories, 55–56
Grace, importance of, 132–34
"Grandpa loves Nick" story, 8–9
Greeks (ancient), 67, 129
Griffin, Susan, 37–38
Grimm, Brothers, 157
Guilt, nature of, 84

Hale, Nathan, 92, 93
Hamlet (fictional character), 74–75,
  139–40
Happiness
  achieving, 130
  pursuit of, 129–30
Hardy, Thomas, 147
Hauerwas, Stanley, 33, 54, 88
Hawthorne, Nathaniel, 96
Healing broken stories, 3, 84–85,
  113–38
Healing power, in community stories,
  114–19, 125, 156
Hector (legendary character), 42, 121
Hemingway, Ernest, 107
Heroes, vs. protagonists, 167–68
Hitler, Adolf, 10, 82, 144
Hobbit, The (Tolkien), 48
Hollywood B movies, 134
Holocaust, 59–60, 94, 98–99, 114,
  119, 145–46
  See also Auschwitz
Horatio (legendary character), 93
House Made of Dawn (Momaday), 24,
  35–36
Humanness, 15–16, 17
  vs. nonhuman elements, 116–19
Hurston, Zora Neale, 120, 143

Ideas, experiencing, 167
I Have a Dream (King), 136
Iliad (Homer), 42

"I Like to Think of Harriet Tubman"
(Griffin), 37, 38
Illusion, 130
Imagination, and possibility, 27–28
Imagined ends, of story, 70, 73, 76–77
Incident, and character, 64
Individualism, 140–42
and community, 150–51
Interrelatedness, in stories, 4, 6
Irving, Washington, 96
Isaac (Hebrew patriarch), 88–89
Isolation, nature of, 152
Israel of Rizhyn, Rabbi, 114

Jack and the Beanstalk (fairy tale), 9
James, Henry, 64, 76
James, William, 12
Janie (fictional character), 120
Jason (legendary character), 72
Jensen, Robert, 139, 140
Jesus Christ, 31–33, 44, 67–68, 71, 89, 90, 92–94, 126, 132
Jewish Passover celebration, 122
Jim (fictional character), 43–45, 47, 54, 63–66, 73, 85, 147, 157
Joan of Arc, 93
John (Bible), 31
Johnson, Lyndon, 62
Johnson, Magic, 118
Jonah (prophet), 91
Jones, John Paul, 92
Joshua (Hebrew leader), 153
Joyce, James, 109
Judeo-Christianity, 75
Jung, Carl, 52
Jungle Jim (fictional character), 93

Kairos, 67, 68, 168
Karamazov, Alyosha (fictional character), 20, 55
Karamazov, Ivan (fictional character), 20
Karenina, Anna (fictional character), 18
Kennedy, John, 14, 62
Kermode, Frank, 57, 66, 67, 69

Khomeini, Ayatollah, 107
Kierkegaard, Sören, 97, 111, 167
King, Martin Luther, Jr., 55, 70–72, 73, 84, 100, 111, 135–36, 157
Kiowas, 23–25, 155
Kittel, Gerhard, 67
Knights of the Round Table (fictional characters), 72
Knowledge
ethical, 30–31
and experience, 26–27, 33
and memory, 37–40
partial, 148–50
personal, 25
story, 30, 35–37
Kolbe, Father Maximilian, 94
Koufax, Sandy, 89, 111

Language, 117–19
Lawrence, D. H., 34
Laws, of communities, 150–51
Lear (legendary king), 122
Lee, Robert E., 81
Leitch, Thomas, 5
Lewis, Wyndham, 108
Lies, as cover, 157
Life, meaning in, 1–4, 21–22, 57–58, 72–76, 149
See also Plot
Life-defining stories, 3, 84, 87, 124–28, 164–65
See also Broken stories, healing
Lincoln, Abraham, 81, 92
Listening, value of, 16, 119–21
Literature, stories of, 20–21
Lord of the Rings, The (Tolkien), 18, 48
"Lost in the Funhouse" (John Barth), 74
Lynip, Arthur, 104

McAdams, Dan, 78, 84
Macbeth (fictional character), 18
MacIntyre, Alasdair, 7, 15, 21, 58, 72, 127, 167
Magic Tignon (fictional character), 9
Magid of Mezritch, 114

Malcolm X, 116
Man for All Seasons, A (Bolt), 150–51
Mantle, Mickey, 81
Marty, Martin, 115, 116, 120
Marx, Karl, 64, 142
Meaning
   in life, 1–4, 21–22, 57–58, 72–76,
     149
   and stories, 85–86
Melville, Herman, 96, 111
Memory
   importance of, 155–56, 157
   and knowledge, 37–40
Metz, Johann Baptist, 39
Middle, of stories, 62–66, 69, 70, 73,
   74, 135
Middle Ages, 143
Midgley, Mary, 144
Milosz, Czeslaw, 139
Mitchell, Henry, 156
Moby Dick (Melville), 42, 151
Momaday, Scott (Tsoai-talee—Rock-
   Tree Boy), 23–25, 27, 35, 100,
   127, 155–56, 158
Monroe, Marilyn, 81
Monstro (fictional character), 91
Moon, Wally, 89
Morality
   and character, 44–48
   criteria of, 90
   paralysis of, 143–47
   See also Good and evil; Right and
     wrong
Moral law, 32–33
Moral reasoning, 65–66, 147
More, Thomas, 150–51
Morrison, Toni, 100, 141, 157
Moses (prophet of Israel), 31
Moshe-Leib of Sasov, Rabbi, 114
Mother Teresa, 108
Moyers, Bill, 118
Murder in the Cathedral (Eliot), 76
Murphy (fictional character), 18
Mysterious Stranger, The (Twain), 97
Myth of Certainty, The (Taylor), 167

Names, The (Momaday), 24
Narratives, 20, 39
   See also Quest narratives
National anthem, ritual of, 122
Nazis. See Holocaust
Nelson, Harriet, 148
Night (Wiesel), 98–99
Nihilism, 142
Nobel Lecture (Solzhenitsyn), 148–49,
   157
Nonhuman elements, vs. humanness,
   116–19
Novels, impact of, 167
Nussbaum, Martha, 34

Objectivity, quest for, 167
O'Connor, Flannery, 97
_One Day in the Life of Ivan
   Denisovich_ (Solzhenitsyn), 148
Opinionatedness, 147–48

Pain, nature of, 62
   See also Suffering, and character
Pap (fictional character), 43, 63
Paradiso (Dante), 110–11
Participation, in stories, 137, 140, 147
   See also Reader participation
Particulars, nature of, 30, 54
Pascal, Blaise, 55, 101, 111
Passivity, and relativism, 145–47
"Pasture, The" (Frost), 16
Pattern and Growth in Personality
   (Allport), 52
Paul, St., 89
Paul Bunyan (mythical character), 9
Performance, of ritual, 121
Personality, vs. character, 2, 41, 51–
   53, 56, 125, 168
Pheoby (fictional character), 120
Pignatano, Joe, 89
Pilgrims, 81
Pinocchio (fictional character), 90, 91
Plot, 1–2, 3, 17, 58–59, 64, 75–76
Poetry, creation of, 121
Pohd-lohk, 24
Popular culture
   character in, 51–53, 56

stories of, 163–64
Possibility, and imagination, 27–28
Postmodernists, 73
Pound, Ezra, 106
Price, Reynolds, 5, 39, 49, 75, 77, 79
Procrustes (legendary character), 129
Protagonists, vs. heroes, 167–68
Proust, Marcel, 105
Proverbs, 19
Prynne, Hester (fictional character),
    31
Pseudo-stories, 14
Psychology, 167
    and guilt, 84
    negativism of, 61
    and self, 51–52
    and values, 168
    See also Gestalt psychology
Public stories, shared, 81–82

Quest narratives, 21–22, 72

Rand, Ayn, 144, 151
Rational abstractions, 168
    See also Reason
Reader participation, 124–25
Reality
    and belief, 116
    explanation for, 140
    vs. fiction, 20
Real world, and stories, 85
Reason, 168
    vs. stories, 28–33, 80–83
Reasoning
    abstract, 33
    moral, 65–66, 147
Relativism, 167
    and individualism, 141
    and moral paralysis, 143-47
    negative effects of, 2–3, 19, 149
    and passivity, 145–47
    of values, 157
Religious stories, 13, 87–90, 92–96,
    103–4, 162–63
Remembering. *See* Memory
Repetition, in ritual, 121–22
Repulski, Rip, 89

Responsibility
    and connectedness, 151–52
    vs. freedom, 142–43
    of storyteller, 115–16
Rheinschmidt, Huckleberry, 45
Rich, Adrienne, 126–27
Right and wrong, 19, 90, 96
Ríos, Albert, 11
Rituals, 58, 121–22
"Roles," variety of, 88
Romans, 132
Root, Michael, 86
Roper (fictional character), 151
Rouse, John, 77

Sartre, Jean-Paul, 41
Saul (king of Hebrews), 132
Sawyer, Tom (fictional character), 66
Schindler, Oskar, 168
Schindler's List (film), 168
School stories, 11–13, 161–62
Science, and objectivity, 167
Self
    and community, 141
    and freedom, 137–38
    making quality of story, 77
    road to healthy, 56
    and psychology, 51–52
Self-delusion, 157
Separateness, overcoming, 152, 157
Sesame Street (TV show), 81
Shah of Iran, 107
Shared stories, 14–15, 116–19, 120–
    22, 133
    See also Public stories, shared
Sheena—Queen of the Jungle
    (fictional character), 93
Significant actions
    in beginnings, 61
    and freedom, 130–32
    in stories, 15, 17, 21–22
Signifying Monkey (fictional
    character), 9
Silko, Leslie Marmon, 100, 122–24
Silone, Ignazio, 119–20, 142
Skepticism, negativity of, 146–47

"Small, Good Thing, A" (Carver), 132–33
Smokey the Bear (fictional character), 34
Snider, Duke, 89, 92
Solzhenitsyn, Alexander, 100, 148–49, 157
Spectators, vs. characters, 3–4, 145–46
Spider Woman (fictional character), 9
"Stanzas from the Grand Chartreuse" (Arnold), 103
Statistics, vs. stories, 72
Stephen (apostle), 89, 93, 111
Stoicism, 67
Stone, Elizabeth, 83
Stories
  adventure, 161
  American success, 129–30, 134
  beginnings of, 60–62, 69, 73
  belief in, 16–17, 29, 116
  broken, healing, 3, 84–85, 113–38
  colliding, 13–14
  community, 114–19, 125, 156
  core, 125
  decline of, 2–3, 139–43
  defending, 79–80
  definition of, 15, 50
  ending of, 69–73, 74, 135
  exchanging, 6–7
  explanations in, 85
  facts vs., 80–83
  family, 8–11, 101–2, 159–61
  functions of, 155
  good, 55–56
  imagined ends of, 70, 73, 76–77
  interrelatedness in, 4, 6
  invitation of, 16
  life-defining, 3, 84, 87, 124–28, 164–65
  of literature, 20–21
  middle of, 62–66, 69, 70, 73, 74, 135
  participation in, 137, 140, 147
  of popular culture, 163–64
  power of, 121–22
  promises of, 61

public, shared, 81–82
purpose of, 3–4, 5–6
and real world, 85
reason vs., 28–33, 80–83
religious, 13, 87–90, 92–96, 103–4, 162–63
retelling, 122
and rituals, 58, 121–22
school, 11–13, 161–62
self-making quality of, 77
shared, 14–15, 116–19, 120–22, 133
significant actions in, 15, 17, 21–22
sources of, 7–8
vs. statistics, 72
teaching of, 1–2
telling aspect of, 15–16
time in, 15, 19–20
"untold," 15
variety of, 141–42
and world view, 98–101
of zeitgeist, 163–64
See also Fairy tales; Pseudo-stories
Story act, 133
Story knowledge, 30, 35–37
Storyteller, responsibility of, 115–16
Suffering, and character, 49–50
See also Pain, nature of
Sun Also Rises, The (Hemingway), 20

Tarzan (fictional character), 93
Television, impact of, 14–15
Tess (fictional character), 147
Their Eyes Were Watching God (Hurston), 120
Thoreau, Henry David, 96, 111, 116–17, 136
Three Pigs (fictional characters), 9
Time
  in stories, 15, 19–20
  value of, 66–68, 116–17
Tolerance, and relativism, 144–45
Tolkien, J. R. R., 17–18, 47–48
Tolstoy, Leo, 96, 111
Town Beyond the Wall, The (Wiesel), 146
Tragedy, 74–75

Transcendence, 68
  of truth, 135–36
Troupe, Quincy, 117–19
Truman, Harry, 62
Truth
  importance of, 129–30, 148–49
  subjectivity of, 144
  transcendence of, 135–36
Truth, Sojourner, 81
Tubman, Harriet, 37, 38
Twain, Mark, 14, 43, 44, 45, 66, 96,
  97, 157

Uncle Remus (fictional character),
  157
Uncle Tom (fictional character), 81
Understanding
  barriers to, 152
  partial, 148–50
  of shared stories, 117–18, 133
Uniqueness, danger of, 152
"Untold stories," 15

Values, 39, 145, 150
  in academic discourse, 168
  crucial, 154
  formation of, 29, 53
  internalizing, 152
  relativism of, 157

Vietnam War, 18, 86, 96
Voltaire, 145
Voyeurism, vs. curiosity, 146

Walker, Alice, 100, 131
War and Peace (Tolstoy), 109–10
Warren, Robert Penn, 1
Weingarten, Mrs., 99
Welty, Eudora, 155
"Where I'm Calling From" (Carver),
  132
Whitehead, Alfred North, 79
Wiesel, Elie, 39, 98–99, 100, 113–14,
  123, 145–46, 157
Wilhelm, Tommy (fictional character),
  18
Wills, Maury, 89
Wisdom, nature of, 150, 156
Woiwode, Larry, 25–26
Wollstonecraft, Mary, 126
Woolf, Virginia, 23
Words, importance of, 119
Wordsworth, William, 61, 121
World view, and stories, 98–101
World War II, 85, 134
Wrong, *See* Right and Wrong

Zeitgeist, stories of, 163–64